# Small Amish Quilt
# PATTERNS

# Small Amish Quilt
# PATTERNS

*For Crib Quilts and Wall Hangings*

## Rachel T. Pellman

Good Books®

Intercourse, PA 17534

## Acknowledgments

We wish to give special thanks to the following persons for their gracious permission to picture their quilts on the covers of this book: left to right—Sunshine and Shadow, Dr. and Mrs. Donald Herr; Rolling Stone, Pat and Kemp Beall; Nine-Patch, collection of Eve and David Wheatcroft, Lewisburg, PA; Log Cabin, collection of Eve and David Wheatcroft; Bear Paw, Pat and Kemp Beall.

Design by Dawn J. Ranck

Photos on cover by Kirk Zutell/BRT Photographic Illustrations.

SMALL AMISH QUILT PATTERNS

Copyright © 1985 by Good Books, Intercourse, PA 17534

First published in 1985 (ISBN: 0-934672-30-X

REVISED EDITION, 1998

International Standard Book Number: 1-56148-236-6

Library of Congress Catalog Card Number: 85-70280

**Library of Congress Cataloging in Publication Data**

Pellman, Rachel T. (Rachel Thomas)
    Small Amish quilt patterns / Rachel T. Pellman. — Intercourse,
Pa. : Good Books, c1985.
        128 p. : chiefly ill. ; 28 cm.
        Bibliography: p. 123-124
        Includes index.
        1. Quilting—Patterns. 2. Quilts, Amish. I. Title
    TT835.P446  1985                    746.9'7041—dc19  85-70280
                                        AACR 2 MARC

# Table of Contents

# How to Use
# *Small Amish Quilt Patterns*

Antique Amish crib quilts are prizes, persistently searched for by collectors. These small treasures are highly valued, bringing prices close to, or exceeding, full-sized antique Amish quilts.

Why are these small quilts so sought after? Why do they bring such high prices? First, these bedcovers are scarce. Fewer crib quilts were made to supply the needs of a household. A quilt could be made for the crib and remain as the crib cover for a series of different occupants. Obviously, such a quilt went through repeated washings. Often they were used until they were thoroughly worn and then thrown out and replaced. Today, collectors are often willing to pay high prices for a crib quilt even if it shows severe signs of wear.

Second, crib quilts are desirable because of their size. They make choice wall displays and are more likely than larger quilts to fit the wall spaces of modern homes.

Crib quilts also carry special feelings. They stand as tangible symbols of love and caring. They hold warm memories of childhood, carefree days, and restful nights, the secure feelings of loving and being loved.

*Small Amish Quilt Patterns* provides the patterns to create these treasures anew. The patterns have been adjusted and refined so that the proportions are pleasing in a small quilt. Templates for piecing, as well as quilting designs, are also given in actual size so that you do not need to adapt them to fit. Though they are suitable for crib quilts, these patterns should not be limited to that. They make startlingly beautiful wallhangings and can be custom-designed to suit any room's color and space needs.

If you choose to create one of these quilts for use as a wallhanging, you know it will not be subjected to the wear and tear that the original crib quilts suffered. So you may piece and quilt with painstaking care and have an heirloom to enjoy.

Or you may choose to create one of these small beauties for a loved child and invest the quilt with hours of tender care.

## Select Pattern and Colors First

Good planning is the most basic rule in successful quiltmaking. It will minimize many frustrations!

You should know before selecting your fabric which quilt pattern you are going to make, how many colors you will need to complete your choice, and which colors or color families you want to use. Since it is difficult to visualize a grouping of colors and fabrics in a quilt when working with either large bolts or small swatches, it is helpful to sketch a scale model of the quilt onto graph paper, and then use crayons or colored pencils to fill in your choice of colors.

## Making a Model

You can get an even more accurate color representation by purchasing small amounts of the fabrics you are considering and cutting them into tiny patches to cover the appropriate areas on your scale model. This is especially helpful when working with those patterns using large geometric shapes. It becomes more tedious when working with patterns involving small patches. Despite that, it is a beneficial exercise since it allows you to see in advance whether one fabric is lost or dominant among the others. If, for instance, you are trying to emphasize a particular design within a patch, the surrounding areas will need to provide adequate contrast so the design pattern will stand out. You achieve this by using light and dark fabrics or contrasting colors.

## Choosing Good Fabric

The quality of a quilt is only as good as the quality of each of its components. Therefore, it is essential to choose high quality fabrics for quiltmaking.

Lightweight 100% cotton or cotton/polyester blends are ideal for quiltmaking. In addition, 100% cottons have a dull finish, making them similar to old fabrics. (Cottons blended with synthetics tend to have more luster or sheen.) The fabric should be tightly woven so it does not ravel excessively. If you check its cut edges and find it frays easily, the fabric will be difficult to work with, especially in small pieces.

Test it for wrinkling by grasping a handful and squeezing it firmly. If sharp creases remain when you release the fabric, it will wrinkle as you work

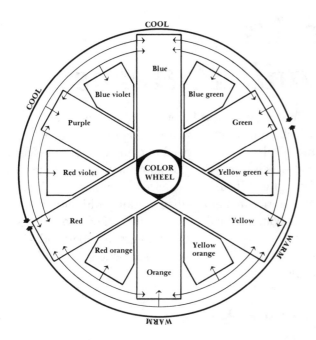

with it and will not have a smooth appearance, especially if it is used in large sections on a quilt.

It is wise to wash all fabrics before using them to preshrink and test them for colorfastness.

## Selecting "Amish" Colors

Historically, most Amish quiltmakers did not understand the science of color selection and combinations. They followed their intuitions and used what was at hand.

In the past and today, Amish homes are bare by most American standards. Walls are generally painted a plain blue or green. Floors, if carpeted at all, are usually covered with handmade rag rugs. Very little upholstered furniture is used. In short, the Amish, because of their commitment to simplicity, have traditionally given very little effort to coordinating room decor and accessories.

The same is true of their clothing. The Amish style of dress is prescribed by the church. They are not concerned about the latest styles or fashionable colors. Consequently, they are not bound by the surrounding culture's sense of what is proper and what is not.

This freedom from the dictates of society's norms is evident in the color schemes of antique Amish quilts. Frequently, the colors which color theory describes as complementary appear together in Amish quilts. Likely the makers never *knew* they had selected complementary colors, but they could *see* that those colors brought out the best in each other.

Many Amish quilts have accents of black and red, a combination that decorators recognize as a boost for many color schemes. When Amish women emptied their scrap bags they didn't work from a basis of scientific knowledge. They just chose fabrics in relation to each other. Many times the result was a dramatic color scheme that stands up well today.

It would be unfair to imply that all Amish quilts demonstrate masterful use of color. Many are less than pleasingly coordinated. But if you want to capture the unusual power of antique Amish quilt colors, you will likely be most successful if you try to forget what you know about color and use a fresh approach.

There are several guidelines you might follow. The fabrics used in antique Amish quilts were almost always of solid colors. Printed fabrics seldom appear. The oldest, most traditional Amish quilts come from eastern Pennsylvania, specifically from Lancaster County. This early settlement tended to be more conservative than some of the groups who later migrated to other areas.

Lancaster Amish primarily used only a part of the spectrum of the color wheel, avoiding warm colors—bright reds, red orange, orange, yellow orange, yellows, and yellow green. The "cool" colors—burgundys, blues, purples, and greens—were the colors they were permitted to use for clothing and also their quilts. Therefore, the more conservative, traditional Amish quilts reflected their community's standards and used a myriad of colors, but only those within the boundaries of that "cooler" spectrum.

Antique Amish quilts made in areas outside eastern Pennsylvania were often more daring in their colors. Yellows and oranges appear frequently in midwestern quilts and those made in Pennsylvania counties other than Lancaster. However, these colors are used in conjunction with the darker hues.

Try, as much as you can, to approach your color selection in an uninhibited way. The closer you can come to that approach, the more likely it is that you can create a quilt that looks authentically Amish.

Experiment with colors in several arrangements before you make a final decision. See how they stand in reference to each other. Some colors highlight one another, and others dull each other.

## Don't Forget Black

To approximate "Amish" color choices, use colors of varying intensities and shades. And don't forget black. Black, although dark, can be a spark of life in a color scheme. Several shades of black may be more interesting than only one. The varying shades that appear in old quilts happened because they were often made with scraps. Substitutions were often made for fabrics that ran out. You should not be afraid to try substituting one or several similar fabrics instead of using the same one throughout the quilt.

Quiltmakers in Lancaster County used black sparingly in their quiltmaking, and thus highlighted other colors in their quilts.

In contrast, quilters in the midwestern Amish communities liked black and used it extensively in their quilts. Frequently they selected black as a background color and used it with pieced blocks of vibrant, contrasting colors, thereby creating a dramatic visual impact.

## Planning Borders

Notice the role that borders play in traditional Amish quilts. At times they served to increase a quilt's dimensions to an adequate size; at other times they acted as the frame that highlighted the quilt pattern. In certain cases they achieved both at the same time. At any rate, a border is never an afterthought. Many Amish quilts have wide, elaborately quilted borders.

The important factor is that the borders should be proportionate to the interior pattern of the quilt. You will notice that border widths vary from pattern to pattern.

## Creating Your Templates

Given with each pattern in this book are templates (and instructions for piecing and connecting individual block units). Trace the templates *accurately* onto a material that will withstand repeated outlining without wearing down the edges.

Cardboard is not appropriate for a template that must be traced repeatedly. More durable materials are plastic lids from throw-away containers—the sides of a plastic milk, water, or bleach jug; old linoleum scraps; or tin. (If you use tin, beware of sharp edges.) You may glue sandpaper to the back of the template to keep it from slipping as you mark the fabrics.

If your template is not accurately traced or cut, you will have a very difficult time making your quilt fit together well.

Before you cut all the quilt's patches, cut enough for just one block using the templates you've made. Assemble the patch to test for accuracy. Be sure to

sew all seams using exactly ¼-inch seam allowances. If you need to make changes, adjust the templates and try again. *Always test the templates by assembling one block before you cut fabrics for an entire quilt top.*

You may make your templates with or without a seam allowance, depending on the method of marking, cutting, and piecing you prefer.

## Marking Patches with *Seam Allowances*

This method requires that the template be made with a ¼-inch seam allowance on all sides. The line that you trace onto the fabric becomes the cutting line. The seam line is ¼-inch inside the marked line. The advantage of this method is that you can trace the outline on the top layer of fabric, and then cut through several layers of fabric at the same time. The disadvantage is that when you begin stitching the patches together, you will need to guess accurately the exact location of the ¼-inch seam allowances so that the corners of the patches meet precisely.

## Marking Patches without Seam Allowances

This method requires that the template be made the actual size of the finished patch. The line that you trace onto the fabric becomes the stitching line. You must imagine the cutting line ¼-inch outside this line. The advantage here is that you have a tracing line to stitch along, almost guaranteeing accuracy in piecing. The disadvantage is that each patch must be marked and cut individually. With this method you cannot stack and cut multiple layers of fabrics. Each quilter must choose which of these methods works best for her/him. The important thing is to maintain accuracy by whatever way you find most comfortable.

It is extremely important to be precise in marking and cutting. A very minute mistake in either step will be multiplied many times over when you try to assemble the quilt. Ultimately, you want to have a smooth, flat quilt top. To achieve that, the individual pieces must fit together precisely.

## Marking Fabrics

There are many ways to mark fabrics. You may use a regular lead pencil to trace the template.

However, on some fabrics, especially dark fabrics, the markings will be very difficult to see.

There are several pencils designed especially for quilters. Some of these make markings that are soluble in cold water, allowing the markings to be easily removed. Some pencils make markings that disappear after a certain period of time. That utensil works well if you use the marked pieces before the time elapses. Whatever you choose, be sure to follow the manufacturer's instructions for the marker's use.

Every quiltmaker should have a good pair of sharp fabric shears. The longer the blade of the scissors, the greater the chances of cutting a continuous straight line. The scissors must be sharp all the way to the point to cut well-defined corners.

## A Word About Rotary Cutters and Strip-Piecing

Some quilters prefer to cut patches without templates, using a rotary cutter and a ruler to measure instead. This method can be faster and more accurate, especially if you are cutting simple shapes like squares and rectangles. If you prefer to use this method, be sure to use the same ruler and mat for all measuring. Rulers vary slightly and can create problems with accuracy if you use more than one ruler in a project.

Although we give instructions for the traditional method of connecting individual patches, you may strip-piece instead. To do that, sew strips of fabric together, and then cut patches in units from the already joined strips. This is particularly useful in patterns such as the Nine-Patch or Roman Stripe.

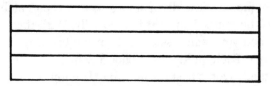

*Join fabric into vertical strips.*

*Cut horizontal units.*

For example, to strip-piece a Nine-Patch block, sew three strips of fabric together to form a vertical strip. Cut the strip horizontally to form units of three patches, which are already joined and ready to be sewn together to form the Nine-Patch block.

To strip-piece a Roman Stripe block, sew the strips together, and then cut the triangles.

*Join vertical strips of fabric.*

*Cut triangle units from joined strips.*

Strip-piecing works more efficiently with some patterns than with others. You will need to determine whether or not you want to make it part of your quiltmaking.

## Piecing

You may piece a quilt by hand or by machine. Hand-piecing is a more time-consuming and laborious process. Most quilters today choose to piece by machine. However, when you are working with very small pieces and when you need to make several points meet, hand-piecing is the most precise and exact method. This way also allows you to work on the project anywhere, rather than being tied to a sewing machine. If you hand-piece, you can still stitch the borders and the sashing between blocks on the sewing machine to save time.

Hand-piecing is very simple. Pin the patches with their right sides together and with their stitching lines perfectly matched. Using a fine sharp needle, stitch with short running stitches through both layers of fabric. Stitches must be straight, even, and tight to achieve an accurate and strong seam. Check the stitches periodically to be sure they are not causing puckering. Put an occasional backstitch in with the running stitches to tighten the seam without creating puckers. At the end of the patch, backstitch and knot the thread before clipping. Open the patch and check the seam for precision.

When piecing, always begin by assembling the smaller patches, and then build them on to larger pieces to form the quilt block. Combine patches to form straight sewing lines whenever you can.

Avoid having to set in squares and triangles if at all possible, since stitching around corners requires the utmost care to prevent bunching and puckering. When setting in is required, stitch the patches that need to be set against each other only to the ends of their stitching lines. Do *not* stitch through their seam allowances. The seam allowances must be kept free to fit against the seam allowances on the pieces being added.

There are two ways to set in a corner. One is to start at the outer edges of one patch, stitch its full length (stopping at the seam allowance), pivot, and proceed along the other edge. The other method is to begin stitching along the edge at the center or inner corner. Stitch from the inner corner to one outside edge and then go back to the corner and stitch the remaining edge. Practice both methods and use the one that works best for you.

Machine-piecing is obviously a lot faster than hand-piecing. The procedure is basically the same as hand-piecing, but the stitching is done by machine. Pin the patches together accurately. Watch carefully that they do not slip as they go through the machine. Backstitch whenever you begin or end a seam.

When you join units of patches to each other, you will face the problem of what to do with the seam allowances. Seam allowances are a particular menace in two situations: one, if quilting needs to be done through the seam allowances making small stitches virtually impossible; and two, if a seam allowance of a dark fabric is visible underneath a lighter fabric.

It is generally a good idea to lay all seam allowances in the same direction. However, if this creates either of the above problems, make an exception and lay the seam allowance the opposite way.

## Preparing to Quilt

Much of the wonder of old Amish quilts is in their quilting. They have been lavished with quilting designs, leaving few open spaces. This tiny, intricate quilting is essential in reproducing the look of an old quilt.

*A quilt is a sandwich of three layers—the quilt back, lining or batting, and the quilt top—all held together by quilting stitches.*

You can mark quilting designs on the quilt top in a variety of ways. See "Marking Fabrics" on page 5 for information about quilt marking pencils. Remember to mark with something that will not rub off easily, because, as you quilt, your hands will move across the surface. At the same time, you want the markings to be completely removable when the quilting is completed, so that unsightly lines do not remain.

If you work with fabric that is light enough to see through, it is easiest to mark by tracing. Outline the quilting designs on paper with a heavy magic marker. Lay the fabric to be marked, wrong side down, on top of the quilting design. Trace with a fabric marker over the lines to stitch.

Although this method is easiest, many fabrics used in Amish quilts are too dark to see the lines through the fabric. Therefore, the design must be traced in an alternate way. You can do this by cutting very thin slashes at intervals on the quilting template. This creates a dot-to-dot effect with the slashes. Lay the template on top of the right side of the fabric and trace the lines onto the quilt top.

Since you will use the templates repeatedly, it is wise to make them of a material more durable than paper. Either cardboard or thin plastic is suitable.

You can mark straight lines or crosshatching by laying a ruler on the fabric and tracing along both sides. On large areas, snap a chalk line across the quilt.

When you just want to outline patches, you do not need to mark around them. Simply quilt close to the seam to emphasize the patch.

*To both secure the quilting thread at the beginning, and to hide the knot, insert the needle through **only** the quilt top, about one inch from where the quilting will begin. Pull the thread through to the knot, and gently tug on the knot until it slips through the fabric and is lodged invisibly underneath the top.*

Quilting is both a descriptive word and an action word. To quilt means to stitch three layers of material together to form a heavier whole. The finished stitches, often done in decorative patterns, are also called quilting.

A quilt is a sandwich of three layers: the quilt back, the lining or batting which adds insulation value, and the top which is often pieced or appliqued. The three layers are held together by the quilting stitches.

## Making Tiny, Even Stitches

To quilt, use a simple running stitch. Quilting is done most easily and durably with quilting thread, since it is heavier than regular thread and more able to withstand being pulled repeatedly through three quilt layers.

Quilting needles are called "betweens." They are shorter than "sharps," which are considered normal handsewing needles. Betweens come in various sizes which are identified by numbers. Most quilters use a size 7 or 8 to quilt. Some quilters prefer the even smaller size 9 needle. The best way to choose a needle size is to try several, and then use the one that seems most comfortable for you.

A thimble is a must for quilting since the needle must be pushed repeatedly through three fabric layers. The thimble should fit snugly on the second finger of the hand used for pushing the quilting needle.

To begin quilting, cut a piece of quilting thread about one yard in length. Thread the needle and make a single knot at the end of the thread. Then insert the needle through *only* the quilt top, about one inch from where quilting will begin. Pull the thread through to the knot. Gently tug on the knot until it slips through the fabric and is lodged invisibly underneath the top. This will secure the quilting thread at the beginning.

With one hand underneath the quilt and the other on top, push the needle through all three layers until the hand underneath feels a prick. That indicates that you've been successful and stitched through all the thicknesses! (Experienced quilters develop calluses from this repeated pricking.)

Then with the thimble on your upper hand, tilt the needle upward. Use your lower hand to push up slightly from underneath. As soon as the needle point appears again on top, reinsert it through the layers again. Continue this process until three to five stitches are stacked on the needle. Finally, pull the needle and thread through the fabric to create the quilting pattern. The stitches should be snug but not so tight as to create puckering. Continue the process of stacking stitches onto the needle until the thread is used.

When the length of thread is nearly gone, do a tiny backstitch to secure the thread. Insert the needle again through only the top layer, and make a stitch the length of the needle, away from the quilting design. Pull the needle through the surface and snip the thread with the long stitch left buried underneath the quilt top. Thread the needle and begin again.

The goal is to strive for tiny, even stitches. And they come only with practice! Initially, concentrate on making straight, *even* stitches, without worrying too much about their size. Try to have the stitch length be the same on both the top and bottom of the quilt. Holding the needle straight is crucial for achieving straight stitches. Then after you have mastered evenness, try to decrease the size of the stitches.

When quilting curved lines, do not try to stack as many stitches on the needle before pulling it through. No more than two stitches on the needle at a time are best for executing smooth, even curves.

The type of batting or lining used in a quilt will affect its finished look. Polyester batting has a much puffier quality than the lining used in antique quilts. Cotton batting creates a flatter, smoother effect and is available from quilt supply shops. A thin sheet blanket, or something similar, adds weight and insulation value but retains the flat appearance of an old quilt. These thinner materials also make it possible to quilt tiny, even stitches.

## Putting the Quilt in the Frame

In order to achieve a smooth, even quilting surface, it is necessary to stretch all three layers of the quilt in a frame. This creates a taut surface conducive to quilting.

The most traditional and probably the most effective frame is the type that is large enough to stretch out the entire quilt at once. This allows for even tension over the whole quilt. These frames are generally used at quiltings when several persons work on the quilt at the same time.

The disadvantages of such a frame are its size and lack of mobility. Since the entire quilt surface is exposed, the frame obviously requires that much floor space. Also, once the quilt is stretched in the frame, it should not be removed until quilting is completed. That usually means that the space is occupied for an extended period of time. Many quilters do not have the space required for such a frame.

Another type of frame accommodates the entire quilt at once, but most of it is rolled on to a long rail along one side of the frame. Only about a three-foot length, along the width of the quilt, is exposed for quilting. As that area is completed, the quilt is rolled on to the opposite rail until the entire quilt is finished.

Still smaller frames are available for quilters with very limited space. These look like giant embroidery hoops which allow the quilt to be quilted in small sections.

A very important procedure before using this type of frame is to baste the entire quilt together through all three layers. Basting should begin at the center and work out towards the edges. Doing this assures that the layers will be evenly stretched while being quilted, and it avoids creating puckers during the quilting process. However, do not quilt over the basting stitches because this makes them extremely tedious to remove later.

## Binding the Quilt

The final step in finishing a quilt is adding its binding. The binding covers the raw edges along the four sides of a quilt. Bindings, particularly on antique Amish quilts from Pennsylvania, are generally wider than bindings found on many other quilts.

Since the edge of a quilt receives a lot of wear, the binding is often done with a double thickness of fabric. It is not uncommon for bindings on old quilts to have been machine-stitched in place.

Bindings can be done in several ways. One of the easier methods is to cut strips of fabric that measure four times the width of the finished binding. These strips can be cut either lengthwise or crosswise on the fabric grain. Lengthwise strips do not need to be pieced, but piecing on a binding is not very obvious and can be done without diminishing the beauty of the quilt.

Cut four binding strips, each one measuring the length of one side of the quilt, plus one inch.

Fold each binding strip in half, wrong sides together, so that both raw edges meet. Trim any excess lining and backing from the quilt itself. Pin the shorter two binding strips against the two parallel edges of the quilt top's width, with the raw edges of the binding flush with the raw edges of the quilt.

Machine-stitch in place using a ¼-inch seam allowance. Open the seam so that the folded edge of the binding is now the outer edge of the quilt.

Sew the remaining binding strips onto the other two sides of the quilt, extending out to the folded edge of the attached binding strips. Fold the binding in half again so that the previously folded edge goes around to the back and covers the seam made by attaching the strips. Handstitch the binding in place. Fold corners under so that no raw edges are exposed.

Another method of finishing a quilt, less commonly used on old Amish designs, is to simply wrap excess border fabric from the top, bottom, and sides of the quilt around to the back where it is stitched in place. Or wrap the extra backing fabric forward over the raw edges to the front, where you can stitch it in place on the quilt top.

Most old Amish quilts used a cut binding. It was frequently in a color which contrasted with the border and was new to the color scheme of the interior of the quilt.

After your binding is completed, it is a good idea to initial and date your quilt so that it can be identified by future generations. You can sign and date it with embroidery on a lower back corner. Or you may choose to quilt your initials and the date in a lower back corner.

# How to Assemble Your Quilt

**DIAGRAM 1**

**DIAGRAM 2**

# *Border Application Diagram*

In the diagrams below, the border templates are assigned different letter designations than in the individual patterns throughout this book. Adapt these instructions to the patterns you choose.

**ASSEMBLY INSTRUCTIONS:** STEP 1—Sew Blocks B to top and bottom of Unit A. STEP 2—Sew Blocks C to sides of Unit A/B. STEP 3—Sew Blocks D to top and bottom of Unit A/B/C. STEP 4—Sew Blocks E to sides of Unit A/B/C/D.

When corner blocks are used, sew them to the ends of the last border pieces (E), and then add the border and blocks as a complete section.

**STEP 1**

**STEP 2**

**STEP 3**

**STEP 4**

# Center Diamond

*Measurements given with seam allowances.*
- A — 10" x 10"; cut 1
- B — 2⁷/₈" x 2⁷/₈"; cut 4
- C — 10" x 2⁷/₈"; cut 4
- D — 11" x 11"; cut 2, cut in half diagonally
- E — 3¹/₂" x 20³/₄"; cut 4
- F — 3¹/₂" x 3¹/₂"; cut 4
- G — 8¹/₂" x 26³/₄"; cut 4
- H — 8¹/₂" x 8¹/₂"; cut 4

### Fabric Requirements

- ☐ — 1¹/₈ yds.
- ■ — ¹/₂ yd.
- ▨ — ³/₈ yd.
- ▨ — ¹/₂ yd.

Backing — 1¹/₈ yds.
Batting—45" x 45"

### Assembly Instructions:

1. Sew one Template C to Template A. Sew another Template C to the other side of Template A.

2. Sew one Template B to one end of Template C. Sew another Template B to the opposite end of Template C. Repeat with the remaining set of Templates B and C.

3. Sew one B/C to the A/C unit. Sew the other B/C unit to the A/C unit.

4. Sew one Template D to each side of the main unit.

5. Follow instructions for the Border Application as explained and shown on page 11 to assemble Templates E, F, G, and H.

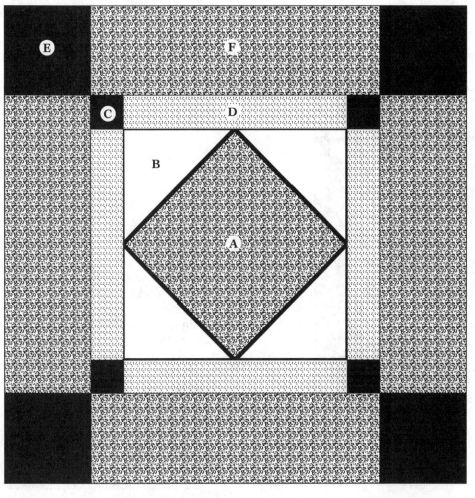

Measurements given with seam allowances.
- A — 15" x 15"; cut 1
- B — 11¹/8" x 11¹/8"; cut 2, then cut in half diagonally
- C — 3¹/2" x 3¹/2"; cut 4
- D — 3¹/2" x 21"; cut 4
- E — 8¹/2" x 8¹/2"; cut 4
- F — 8¹/2" x 27; cut 4

**Fabric Requirements**

☐ — ³/8 yd.

■ — ¹/2 yd.

▦ — 1⁵/8 yds.

▦ — ¹/4 yd.

Backing — 1¹/8 yds.
Batting—45" x 45"

### Assembly Instructions:
1. Sew 4 Template B's to A on 4 sides.
2. Follow instructions for the Border Application as explained and shown on page 11, to assemble Templates C through F.

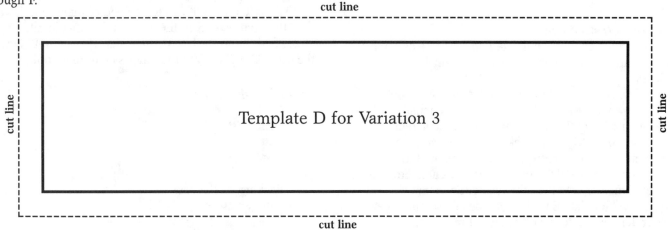

cut line

cut line · cut line

Template D for Variation 3

cut line

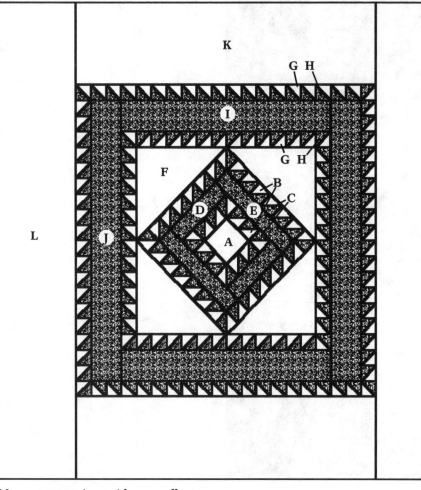

7. Sew 2 strips of 6 blocks and 2 strips of 8 blocks.

8. Sew one strip of 6 blocks to end of main unit. Sew the other strip of 6 blocks to the other end of main unit.

9. Sew one strip of 8 blocks to side of main unit. Sew other strip of 8 blocks to other side of main unit.

10. Sew 4 triangle F's to 4 sides of main unit.

11. Sew long side of Template G to long side of Template H to form square. Repeat with remaining G and H pieces.

12. Sew 2 strips of 12 blocks and 2 strips of 14 blocks.

13. Sew one strip of 12 blocks to end of main unit. Sew the other strip of 12 blocks to the other end of main unit.

14. Sew one strip of 14 blocks to side of main unit. Sew other strip of 14 blocks to other side of main unit.

15. Sew Template I to the one end of main unit. Sew the other Template I to the other end of main unit.

16. Sew Template J to the one side of main unit. Sew the other Template J to the other side of main unit.

17. Sew 2 strips of 18 blocks and 2 strips of 20 blocks.

18. Sew one strip of 18 blocks to end of main unit. Sew other strip of 18 blocks to other end of main unit.

19. Sew one strip of 20 blocks to side of main unit. Sew the other strip of 20 blocks to the other side of main unit.

20. Sew Template K to the one end of main unit. Sew the other Template K to the other end of main unit.

21. Sew Template L to the one side of main unit. Sew the other Template L to the other side of main unit.

*Measurements given with seam allowances.*

A — Template given; cut 1
B — Template given; cut 40
C — Template given; cut 40
D — Template given; cut 2
E — Template given; cut 2
F — 9⁷/₈" x 9⁷/₈"; cut 2, cut in half diagonally
G — 2⁷/₈" x 2⁷/₈"; cut 64, cut in half diagonally
H — 2⁷/₈" x 2⁷/₈"; cut 64, cut in half diagonally
I — 3¹/₂" x 21¹/₂" cut 2
J — 3¹/₂" x 27¹/₂"; cut 2
K — 8¹/₂" x 30¹/₂"; cut 2
L — 8¹/₂" x 46¹/₂; cut 2

### Assembly Instructions:

1. Sew long side of Template B to long side of Template C to form a square block. Repeat with remaining B and C pieces.

2. Sew 2 strips of 2 blocks and 2 strips of 4 blocks.

3. Sew one strip of 2 blocks to end of Template A. Sew the other strip of 2 blocks to the other end of Template A.

4. Sew one strip of 4 blocks to side of main unit. Sew other strip of 4 blocks to other side of main unit.

5. Sew Template D to one end of main unit. Sew the other Template D to the other end of main unit.

6. Sew Template E to the one side of main unit. Sew other Template E to the other side of main unit.

### Fabric Requirements

☐ — 3³/₄ yds.

▩ — 1¹/₈ yds.

Backing — 2¹/₂ yds.
Batting—49" x 49"

Template A

Templates
B and C

Template E

cut line

cut line

cut line

cut line

cut line

cut line

cut line

cut line

cut line

cut line

cut line

cut line

cut line

15

# Sunshine and Shadow

*Measurements given with seam allowances.*

- A — 2" x 2"; cut 57
- B — 2" x 2"; cut 60
- C — 2" x 2"; cut 64
- D — 2" x 2"; cut 64
- E — 2" x 2"; cut 60
- F — 2" x 2"; cut 56
- G — 3¹/2" x 29; cut 2
- H — 3¹/2" x 35; cut 2
- I — 8¹/2" x 35"; cut 4
- J — 8¹/2" x 8¹/2"; cut 4

### Assembly Instructions:

1. Sew Block A to Block B. Sew Blocks C, D, E, and F to A/B to form strip. Continue sewing strips of patches in order as shown in diagram.

2. Sew together strips of patches to form block that is 35" x 35".

3. To assemble Templates G through J, follow instructions for the Border Application as explained on page 11.

### Fabric Requirements

- ⬛ — ¹/4 yd.
- ⬜ — 1¹/8 yds.
- ▦ — 5/8 yd.
- ▦ — ¹/4 yd.
- ▦ — ¹/4 yd.
- ▦ — ¹/4 yd.
- ▧ — ¹/4 yd.

Backing — 2³/4 yds.
Batting—53" x 53"

**Measurements given with seam allowances.**

A — Template given; cut 5
B — Template given; cut 16
C — Template given; cut 28
D — Template given; cut 40
E — Template given; cut 52
F — Template given; cut 20
G — Template given; cut 4
H — Template given; cut 20
I — 15³/4" x 2³/4"; cut 2
J — 20¹/4" x 2³/4"; cut 2
K — Template given; cut 4
L — Template given; cut 40
M — 32/2" x 28¹/2"; cut 2
N — 3¹/2" x 34¹/2"; cut 2
O — 8¹/2" x 34¹/2"; cut 2
P — 8¹/2" x 8¹/2"; cut 2

### Assembly Instructions:

1. Sew Template A to Template B. Sew Templates C, D, E, F, G, and H to A/B to form strip. Continue sewing strips of patches in order as shown in diagram.

2. Sew together strips of patches to form block in center and triangles in corners.

3. Sew one Template I to one side of center unit. Sew other Template I to opposite side.

4. Sew one Template J to one side of center block. Sew other Template J to the opposite side.

5. Sew a triangle of patches in strips to each side of main unit.

6. See Border Application Diagram on page 11 to complete the quilt and use Templates M through P.

### Fabric Requirements

— ⁵/8 yd.
— 1³/8 yd.
— 1/4 yd.
— 1¹/2 yd.
— 3/8 yd.
— 1/4 yd.

Backing — 2³/4 yds.
Batting—53" x 53"

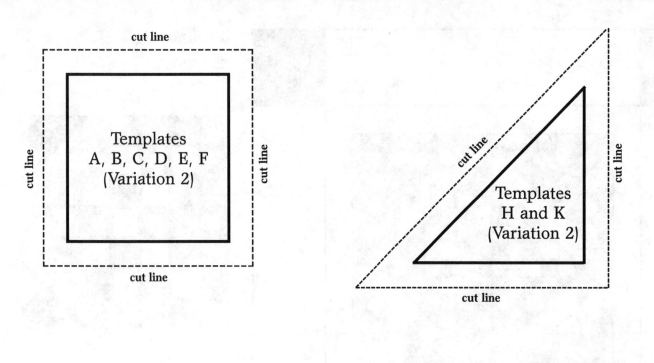

cut line

cut line

Templates
A, B, C, D, E, F
(Variation 2)

cut line

cut line

Templates
H and K
(Variation 2)

cut line

cut line

cut line

Templates G and L
(Variation 2)

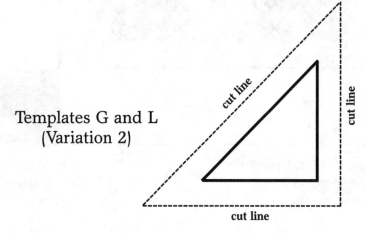

cut line

cut line

cut line

**Measurements given with seam allowances.**

A — 2" x 2"; cut 73

B — 2" x 2"; cut 84

C — 2" x 2"; cut 40

D — 2" x 2"; cut 48

E — 2" x 2"; cut 56

F — 2" x 2"; cut 64

G — Template given; cut 4

H — 2³/8" x 2³/8"; cut 26; then cut in half diagonally

I — 3¹/2" x 30¹/4"; cut 4

J — 3¹/2" x 3¹/2"; cut 4

K — 8¹/2" x 36¹/4"; cut 4

L — 8¹/2" x 8¹/2"; cut 4

### Assembly Instructions:

1. Sew Template A to Template B. Sew Templates C, D, E, F, A, B, G to A/B to form strip. Continue sewing strips of patches in order as shown in diagram.

2. Sew together strips of patches to form block.

3. See Border Application Diagram on page 11 to complete the quilt top, using Templates I through L.

### Fabric Requirements

| | |
|---|---|
| ■ | — ⁵/8 yd. |
| □ | — ¹/2 yd. |
| ▦ | — 1¹/2 yds. |
| ▦ | — ³/8 yd. |
| ▨ | — ¹/4 yd. |
| ▦ | — ³/4 yd. |

Backing — 2⁷/8 yds.

Batting—55" x 55"

Template G

# Bars

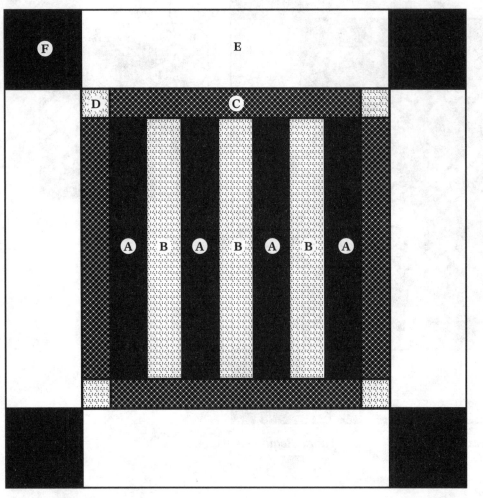

*Measurements given with seam allowances.*
- A — 4¹/4" x 26³/4"; cut 4
- B — 4¹/4" x 26³/4"; cut 3
- C — 3¹/2" x 26³/4"; cut 4
- D — 3¹/2" x 3¹/2"; cut 4
- E — 8¹/2" x 32³/4"; cut 4
- F — 8¹/2" x 8¹/2"; cut 4

## Assembly Instructions:

1. Sew one Template A to one Template B. Sew another Template A to unit A,B. Sew another Template B to unit A,B,A. Sew another Template A to unit A,B,A,B. Sew another Template B to unit A,B,A,B,A. Sew remaining Template A to unit A,B,A,B,A,B.

2. See Border Application Diagram on page 11 to complete the borders using Templates C through F.

## Fabric Requirements

- ◼ — 7/8 yd.
- ◻ — 1 yd.
- ▦ — 3/8 yd.
- ▨ — 1/2 yd.

Backing — 2⁵/8 yds.
Batting—51" x 51"

*Measurements given with seam allowances.*

    A — 5" x 32"; cut 4
    B — 5" x 32"; cut 3
    C — 8¹/₂" x 32; cut 4
    D — 8¹/₂" x 8¹/₂; cut 4

### Assembly Instructions:

1. Sew one Template A to one Template B. Sew another Template A to unit A,B. Sew another Template B to unit A,B,A. Sew another Template A to unit A,B,A,B. Sew another Template B to unit A,B,A,B,A. Sew remaining Template A to unit A,B,A,B,A,B.

2. See Border Application Diagram on page 11 to complete the borders using Templates C and D.

**Fabric Requirements**

    — ³/₄ yd.
    — 1 yd.
    — ⁵/₈ yd.

Backing — 2⁵/₈ yds.
Batting—50" x 50"

## Variation 3

57" x 47"

*Measurements given with seam allowances.*

A — Template given; cut 120
B — Template given; cut 240
C — 5$\frac{1}{2}$" x 35$\frac{1}{2}$"; cut 3
D — 3$\frac{1}{2}$" x 25$\frac{1}{2}$"; cut 2
E — 3$\frac{1}{2}$" x 41$\frac{1}{2}$"; cut 2
F — 8$\frac{1}{2}$" x 31$\frac{1}{2}$"; cut 2
G — 8$\frac{1}{2}$" x 57$\frac{1}{2}$"; cut 2

### Assembly Instructions:

1. Sew two Template Bs to a Template A to creat a horizontal rectangle. Repeat with remaining Templates A and B.

2. Sew 30 A/B units together. Repeat, making a total of 4 strips.

3. Sew one strip to a Template C. Repeat as shown on diagram, until all strips and all Template C's are sewn together.

4. See Border Application Diagram on page 11 to complete the border, using Templates D through G.

### Fabric Requirements

■ — $\frac{1}{2}$ yd.
□ — 1 yd.
▦ — 3$\frac{3}{4}$ yds.

Backing— If using horizontal seams—3$\frac{1}{8}$ yds.
          If using vertical seams—2$\frac{5}{8}$ yds.
Batting— 50" x 60"

22

# Multiple Patch

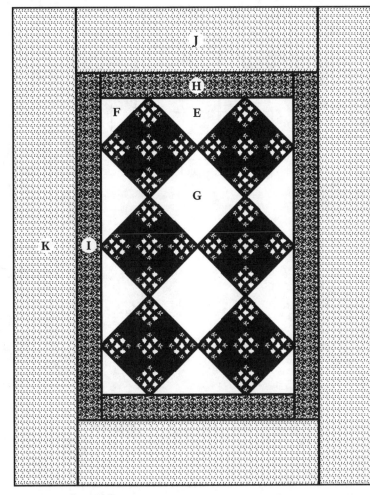

## Variation 1
*46" x 58"*

Measurements given with seam allowances.

A — Template given; cut 30
B — Template given; cut 120
C — Template given; cut 120
D — Template given; cut 24
E — 9³/₈" x 9³/₈"; cut 3; then cut in half diagonally
F — 6⁷/₈" x 6⁷/₈"; cut 2; then cut in half diagonally
G — 9" x 9"; cut 2
H — 3¹/₂" x 24¹/₂"; cut 2
I — 3¹/₂" x 42¹/₂"; cut 2
J — 8¹/₂" x 30¹/₂"; cut 2
K — 8¹/₂" x 58¹/₂"; cut 2

## Assembly Instructions:

1. To create a Multiple Patch Block:

A. Sew a Template C to end of Template B. Sew another Template C to the other end of Template B. Repeat, to make 2 strips.

B. Sew a Template B to end of Template A. Sew another Template B to the other end of Template A.

C. Sew Unit C/B/C to one side of B/A/B. Sew another Unit C/B/C to opposite sides of B/A/B, to form a Multiple Patch block.

D. Sew a Multiple Patch Block to each end of a Template D to create a Strip 1. Repeat, to make 2 Strip 1's.

E. Sew a Template D to each end of a Multiple Patch Block to create a Strip 2.

F. Create a Big Block by sewing a Strip 2 between two Strips 1's.

2. Repeat 5 more times, to create 6 Big Blocks.

3. Follow the diagram, How to Assemble Your Quilt, Diagram 2, on page 10.

4. When your patches are sewn together, follow the Border Application Diagram on page 11, to use Templates H through K.

## Fabric Requirements

— ¹/₂ yd.

— 1¹/₄ yds.

— 2³/₈ yds.

— ³/₄ yd.

Backing — If using horizontal seams—3¹/₄ yds.
          If using vertical seams—2¹/₂ yds.
Batting— 49" x 61"

Template D
(Variation 1)

Templates A, B, C
(Variation 1)

24

## Variation 2

*47" x 57"*

*Measurements given with seam allowances.*

- A — 1³/4" x 1³/4"; cut 72
- B — 1³/4" x 1³/4"; cut 72
- C — 3" x 3"; cut 36
- D — 5¹/2" x 5¹/2"; cut 17
- E — 3¹/2" x 25¹/2"; cut 2
- F — 3¹/2" x 41¹/2"; cut 2
- G — 8¹/2" x 31¹/2"; cut 2
- H — 8¹/2" x 57¹/2"; cut 2

### Assembly Instructions:

1. To create one Multiple Patch Block:

   A. Sew Template A to end of Template B. Repeat 3 times to create 4 strips.

   B. Sew Unit A/B to Unit B/A to form block. Repeat to make 2 blocks.

   C. Sew Template C to block. Repeat to make 2 strips.

   D. Sew two strips together to form block.

2. Repeat entire process 17 more times (18 blocks total).

3. Follow the diagram, How to Assemble Your Quilt, Diagram 2, on page 10.

4. When your patches are sewn together, follow the Border Application Diagram on page 11 to use Templates E through H.

### Fabric Requirements

- ■ — ¹/2 yd.
- □ — 1¹/8 yds.
- ▨ — ¹/2 yd.
- ▨ — ¹/2 yd.

Backing — If using horizontal seams—3¹/8 yds.
If using vertical seams 2⁵/8 yds.

Batting — 50" x 60"

# Irish Chain

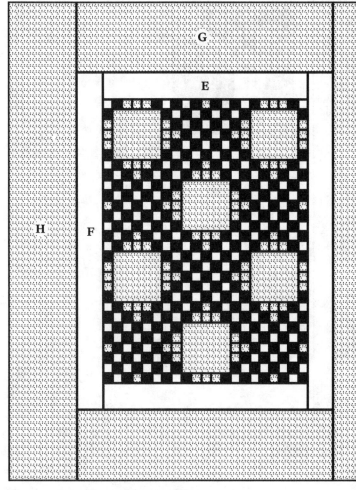

## Variation 1

*46" x 54"*

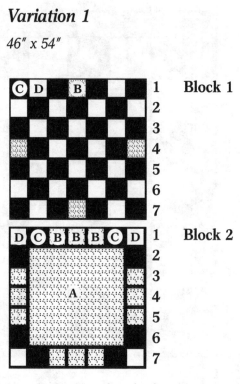

Block 1

Block 2

B. Sew together the first blocks in Rows 2, 3, 4, 5, 6.

C. Sew together the last blocks in Rows 2, 3, 4, 5, and 6.

D. Sew these two strips to either side of Template A.

E. Sew together Row Seven, working from left to right.

F. Sew Row One to top of main block and Row Seven to bottom of main block.

4. Repeat process for Block 2, 5 more times (6 blocks total).

5. Follow the diagram, How to Assemble your Quilt, Diagram 1, on page 10.

6. When your patches are sewn together, follow the Border Application Diagram on page 11 to use Templates E through H.

### Fabric Requirements

— 3/8 yd.

— 7/8 yd.

— 2 3/4 yds.

Backing — If using horizontal seams—3 yds.
           If using vertical seams—2 1/2 yds.
Batting— 49" x 57"

*Measurements given with seam allowances.*

A — Template given; cut 6
B — Template given; cut 144
C — Template given; cut 198
D — Template given; cut 168
E — 3 1/2" x 24 1/2"; cut 2
F — 3 1/2" x 38 1/2"; cut 2
G — 8 1/2" x 30 1/2"; cut 2
H — 8 1/2" x 54 1/2"; cut 2

### Assembly Instructions:

1. To create one Irish Chain Block 1:
   A. Sew together Row One, working from left to right.
   B. Sew together Row Two, working from left to right.
   C. Sew together other 5 rows in Block 1.
   D. Sew Row One to Row Two.
   E. Sew Row Three to other side of Row Two.
   F. Repeat with remaining 5 rows.

2. Repeat process for Block 1, 5 more times (6 blocks total).

3. To create one Irish Chain Block 2:
   A. Sew together Row One, working from left to right.

26

cut line

cut line

cut line

Template A
(Variation 1)

cut line

Templates B, C, D
(Variation 1)

cut line

cut line

cut line

cut line

Templates
A, B, C

(Variation 2)

cut line

cut line

cut line

cut line

*Measurements given with seam allowances.*

A — Template given; cut 108
B — Template given; cut 144
C — Template given; cut 48
D — 6⁷/₈" x 6⁷/₈"; cut 5; then cut in half diagonally
E — 5¹/₈" x 5¹/₈"; cut 2; then cut in half diagonally
F — 6¹/₂" x 6¹/₂"; cut 6
G — 3¹/₂" x 26"; cut 2
H — 3¹/₂" x 40¹/₂"; cut 2
I — 8¹/₂" x 32"; cut 2
J — 8¹/₂" x 56¹/₂"; cut 2

### Assembly Instructions:

1. To create one Irish Chain Block:

A. Sew together Row One, working from left to right. Make a second Row One.

B. Sew together Row Two, working from left to right. Make a second Row Two.

C. Make one Row Three.

D. Sew one Row One and one Row Two together.

E. Sew Row Three to other side of Row Two.

F. Continue with remaining 2 Rows.

2. Repeat 11 more times (12 blocks total).

3. Follow the diagram, How to Assemble your Quilt, Diagram 2, on page 10.

4. When your patches are sewn together, follow the Border Application Diagram on page 11 to use Templates G through J.

### Fabric Requirements

■ — ³/₈ yd.

□ — 3¹/₄ yds.

▨ — 1 yd.

Backing — If using horizontal seams—3¹/₈ yds.
If using vertical seams—2⁵/₈ yds.

Batting— 50" x 59"

# Log Cabin

*46" x 54"*

## Assembly Instructions:

1. To create The Log Cabin Block:

   A. Sew Template B to one side of Template A.

   B. Sew Template C to unit A/B.

   C. Sew Template D to unit A/B/C.

   D. Repeat with strips E through Q until Log Cabin block is formed.

2. Repeat 11 more times (12 blocks total).

3. Follow the diagram, How to Assemble your Quilt, Diagram 1, on page 10.

4. When your patches are sewn together, follow the Border Application Diagram on page 11 to use Templates R through U.

*Measurements given with seam allowances.*

A — Template given; cut 12
B — Template given; cut 12
C — Template given; cut 12
D — Template given; cut 12
E — Template given; cut 12
F — Template given; cut 12
G — Template given; cut 12
H — Template given; cut 12
I — Template given; cut 12
J — Template given; cut 12
K — Template given; cut 12
L — Template given; cut 12
M — Template given; cut 12
N — Template given; cut 12
O — Template given; cut 12
P — Template given; cut 12
Q — Template given; cut 12
R — 3½" x 24½"; cut 2
S — 3½" x 38½"; cut 2
T — 8½" x 30½"; cut 2
U — 8½" x 54½"; cut 2

## Fabric Requirements

— ⅛ yd.

— 2¼ yds.

— ⅛ yd.

— ⅝ yd.

— ⅛ yd.

— ¼ yd.

— ⅛ yd.

— ¼ yd.

— ⅛ yd.

Backing — If using horizontal seams—3 yds.
If using vertical seams—2½ yds.
Batting— 49" x 57"

30

31

# Rail Fence

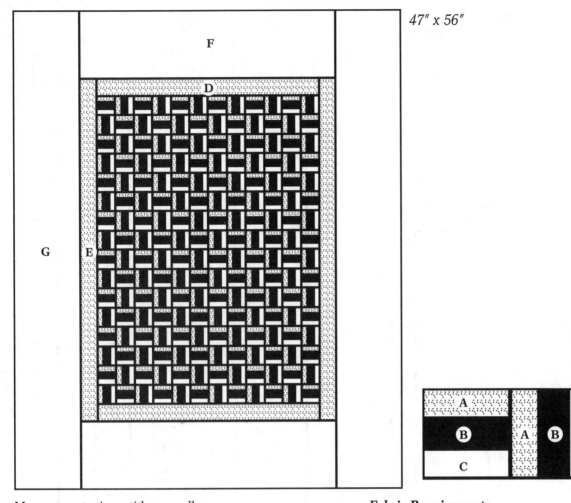

47" x 56"

Measurements given with seam allowances.

A — 1¹/4" x 2³/4"; cut 192
B — 1¹/4" x 2³/4"; cut 192
C — 1¹/4" x 2³/4"; cut 192
D — 2¹/2" x 27¹/2"; cut 2
E — 2¹/2" x 40¹/2"; cut 2
F — 8¹/2" x 31¹/2"; cut 2
G — 8¹/2" x 56¹/2"; cut 2

## Assembly Instructions:

1. Sew one Template A to one Template B. Sew Template C to unit A/B. Repeat 191 more times (192 blocks total).

2. Sew together A/B/C Units to form strips as shown on diagram above.

3. Sew strips together.

4. Follow Border Application Diagram on page 11 to complete your quilt, using Templates D through G.

## Fabric Requirements

⬛ — ¹/2 yd.

⬜ — 2³/8 yds.

▫ — 3/4 yd.

Backing — If using horizontal seams—3¹/8 yds.
           If using vertical seams—2⁵/8 yds.

Batting— 50" x 59"

32

# Double T

*45¹/2" x 58¹/8"*

*Measurements given with seam allowances.*

- A — 3¹/2" x 3¹/2"; cut 6
- B — 2³/8" x 2³/8"; cut 48; then cut in half diagonally
- C — 2³/8" x 2³/8"; cut 48; then cut in half diagonally
- D — 3⁷/8" x 3⁷/8"; cut 12; then cut in half diagonally
- E — 3⁷/8" x 3⁷/8"; cut 12; then cut in half diagonally
- F — 7¹/4" x 7¹/4"; cut 2; then cut in half diagonally
- G — 9⁷/8" x 9⁷/8", cut 3; then cut in half diagonally
- H — 9¹/2" x 9¹/2"; cut 2
- I — 2¹/2" x 24¹/2"; cut 2
- J — 2¹/2" x 42⁵/8"; cut 2
- K — 8¹/2" x 30"; cut 2
- L — 8¹/2" x 58⁵/8"; cut 2

## Assembly Instructions:

1. To create one Double T block:

A. Sew long side of Template B to long side of Template C. Repeat 15 more times (16 B/C Units total).

B. Sew 2 B/C strips together as shown in Block above. Repeat 7 more times (8 B/C strips total). Sew 1 B/C strip to another B/C strips. Repeat 3 more times (4 blocks total).

C. Sew 1 E/D Unit to 1 B/C block. Sew another E/D Unit to the opposite side of the B/C block. Repeat.

D. Sew 1 B/C block to Template A. Sew another B/C unit to opposite side of Template A.

E. Sew three strips together to form block.

F. Repeat entire process 5 more times (6 blocks total).

2. Follow How to Assemble Your Quilt, Diagram 2, on page 10.

3. Follow Border Application Diagram on page 11 to use Templates I through L.

## Fabric Requirements

- □ — 1¹/8 yds.
- ▒ — 2³/4 yds.
- ▓ — 1³/8 yds.

Backing — If using horizontal seams—3¹/4 yds.
If using vertical seams—2¹/2 yds.
Batting— 49" x 61"

33

# Stars

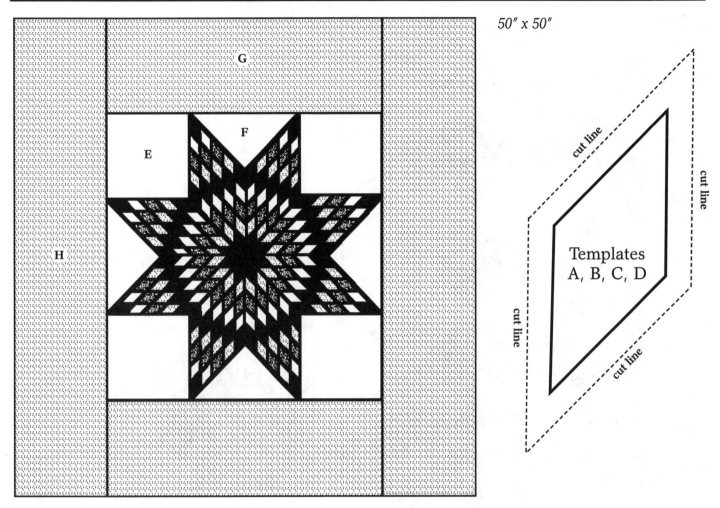

*50" x 50"*

**Templates A, B, C, D**

cut line

*Measurements given with seam allowances.*

A — Template given; cut 56
B — Template given; cut 48
C — Template given; cut 48
D — Template given; cut 48
E — 9$1/2$" x 9$1/2$"; cut 4
F — 9$3/8$" x 9$3/8$"; cut 2;
    then cut in half diagonally
G — 10$1/2$" x 30$1/2$"; cut 2
H — 10$1/2$" x 50$1/2$"; cut 2

### Fabric Requirements

■ — $1/4$ yd.

□ — 1 yd.

▦ — 2$1/4$ yds.

▨ — $1/4$ yd.

Backing — 2$3/4$ yds.; Batting—53" x 53"

### Assembly Instructions:

1. To form one Star block:

A. Sew Template A to Template B. Sew Template C to Unit A/B. Sew Template D to Unit A/B/C. Sew another Template A to Unit A/B/C/D. Repeat. (2 strips total).

B. Sew together a strip of 5 diamonds, starting with B and ending with B.

C. Sew together a strip of 5 diamonds, starting with C and ending with C.

D. Sew together a strip of 5 diamonds, starting with D and ending with D.

E. Sew together 5 strips, as shown, to create large diamond.

F. Repeat entire process 7 more times, to create a total of 8 large diamonds.

2. Sew together 4 large diamonds as shown. Repeat. Sew 2 strips of diamonds together.

3. Insert 4 Template E's into corners.

4. Insert 4 Template F's into sides.

5. Sew Template G to top of center square.

6. Follow Border Application Diagram on page 11 to complete the quilt using Templates G and H.

# Jacob's Ladder

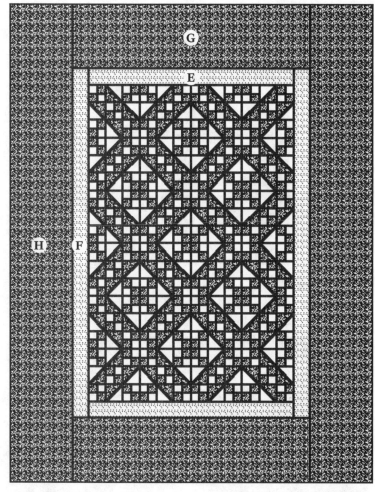

46" x 59"

Templates
C and D

cut line

cut line

cut line

cut line

cut line

cut line

cut line

Templates
A and B

*Measurements given with seam allowances.*

A — Template given; cut 240
B — Template given; cut 240
C — Template given; cut 96
D — Template given; cut 96
E — 2¹/2" x 26¹/2"; cut 2
F — 2¹/2" x 43¹/2"; cut 2
G — 8¹/2" x 30¹/2"; cut 2
H — 8¹/2" x 59¹/2"; cut 2

## Fabric Requirements

— 1¹/8 yds.

— ¹/2 yd.

— ¹/2 yd.

Backing — If using horizontal seams—3¹/4 yds.
          If using vertical seams—2¹/2 yds.
Batting— 49" x 62"

## Assembly Instructions:

1. To form one Jacob's Ladder block:
    A. Sew Template A to Template B. Repeat.
    B. Sew together Unit A/B with Unit B/A to form block. Repeat 4 more times. (5 blocks total).
    C. Sew long side of Template C to long side of Template D. Repeat 3 more times. (4 blocks total.)
    D. Sew A/B Block, to one side of C/D Unit. Sew another A/B Block to opposite side of C/D Unit. Repeat.
    E. Sew C/D Unit to one side of A/B Unit. Sew another C/D Unit to opposite side of A/B Unit.
    F. Sew three strips together to form block.
2. Repeat 23 more times. (24 blocks total.)
3. See How to Assemble Your Quilt, Diagram 1, page 10.
4. Follow Border Application Diagram on page 11 to complete quilt using Templates E through H.

# Baskets

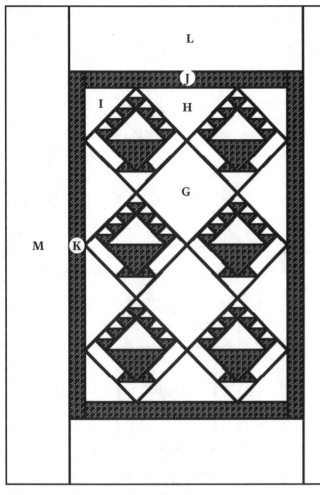

## Variation 1

*45¹/₂" x 58¹/₈"*

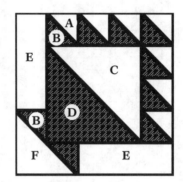

### Assembly Instructions:

1. To form one Basket Block:

A. Sew the long side of Template A to the long side of Template B. Repeat 6 times (7 blocks total).

B. Sew the long side of Template C to the long side of Template D.

C. Sew together 4 of the A/B Units to form a horizontal strip.

D. Sew together 3 of the A/B Units to form a vertical strip.

E. Sew Unit C/D to vertical strip of 3 A/B Units.

F. Sew horizontal strip of 4 A/B Units to A/B/C/D Unit to create block.

G. Sew Template B to end of Template E. Sew another Template B to end of another Template E.

H. Sew B/E Unit to bottom of large block. Sew second B/E Unit to left side of large block.

I. Sew Template F to corner of large unit to create Basket Block.

2. Repeat 5 more times (6 blocks total).

3. See How to Assemble Your Quilt, Diagram 2, on page 10.

4. Follow Border Application Diagram on page 11 to complete your quilt, using Templates J through M.

*Measurements given with seam allowances.*

A — Template given; cut 42
B — Template given; cut 54
C — 6¹/₄" x 6¹/₄"; cut 3; then cut in half diagonally
D — 6¹/₄" x 6¹/₄"; cut 3; then cut in half diagonally
E — Template given; cut 12
F — Template given; cut 6
G — 9¹/₂" x 9¹/₂"; cut 2
H — 9⁷/₈" x 9⁷/₈"; cut 3; then cut in half diagonally
I — 7¹/₄" x 7¹/₄"; cut 2; then cut in half diagonally
J — 2¹/₂" x 26"; cut 2
K — 2¹/₂" x 42⁵/₈"; cut 2
L — 8¹/₂" x 30"; cut 2
M — 8¹/₂" x 58⁵/₈"; cut 2

### Fabric Requirements

□ — 1¹/₈ yds.

▒ —1³/₈ yds.

▓ — 4 yds.

Backing — If using horizontal seams—3¹/₄ yds.
If using vertical seams—2¹/₂ yds.
Batting— 48" x 61"

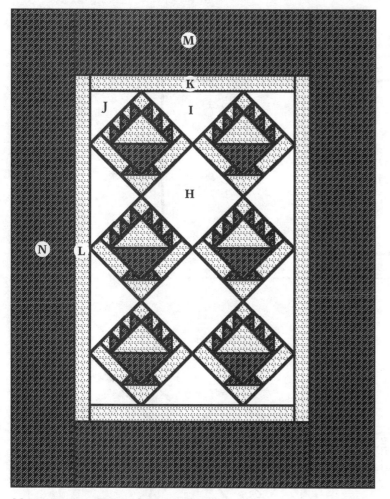

## Variation 2

*45½" x 58⅛"*

*Measurements given with seam allowances.*

A — Template given; cut 48
B — Template given; cut 36
C — 6¼" x 6¼"; cut 3; then cut in half diagonally
D — 6¼" x 6¼"; cut 3; then cut in half diagonally
E — Template given; cut 12
F — Template given; cut 6
G — Template given; cut 6
H — 9½" x 9½"; cut 2
I — 9⅞" x 9⅞"; cut 3; then cut in half diagonally
J — 7¼" x 7¼"; cut 2; then cut in half diagonally
K — 2½" x 26"; cut 2
L — 2½" x 42⅝"; cut 2
M — 8½" x 30"; cut 2
N — 8½" x 58⅝", cut 2

### Assembly Instructions:

1. To form one Basket Block:

A. Sew the long side of Template A to the long side of Template B. Repeat 5 times (6 blocks total).

B. Sew the long side of Template C to the long side of Template D.

C. Sew together 3 of the A/B Units to form a horizontal strip. Repeat to form a vertical strip.

D. Sew Template G to end of vertical strip.

E. Sew Unit C/D to horizontal strip of 3 A/B Units.

F. Sew vertical strip to A/B/C/D Unit to create block.

G. Sew Template A to end of Template E. Sew another Template A to end of another Template E.

H. Sew A/E Unit to bottom of large block. Sew second A/E Unit to left of large block.

I. Sew Template F to corner of large unit to create Basket Block.

2. Repeat 5 more times (6 blocks total).

3. See How to Assemble Your Quilt, Diagram 2, on page 10.

4. Follow Border Application Diagram on page 11 to complete your quilt, using Templates K through N.

### Fabric Requirements

☐ — 1⅛ yds.

▨ — ½ yd.

Backing — If using horizontal seams—3¼ yds.
            If using vertical seams—2½ yds.
Batting— 48" x 61"

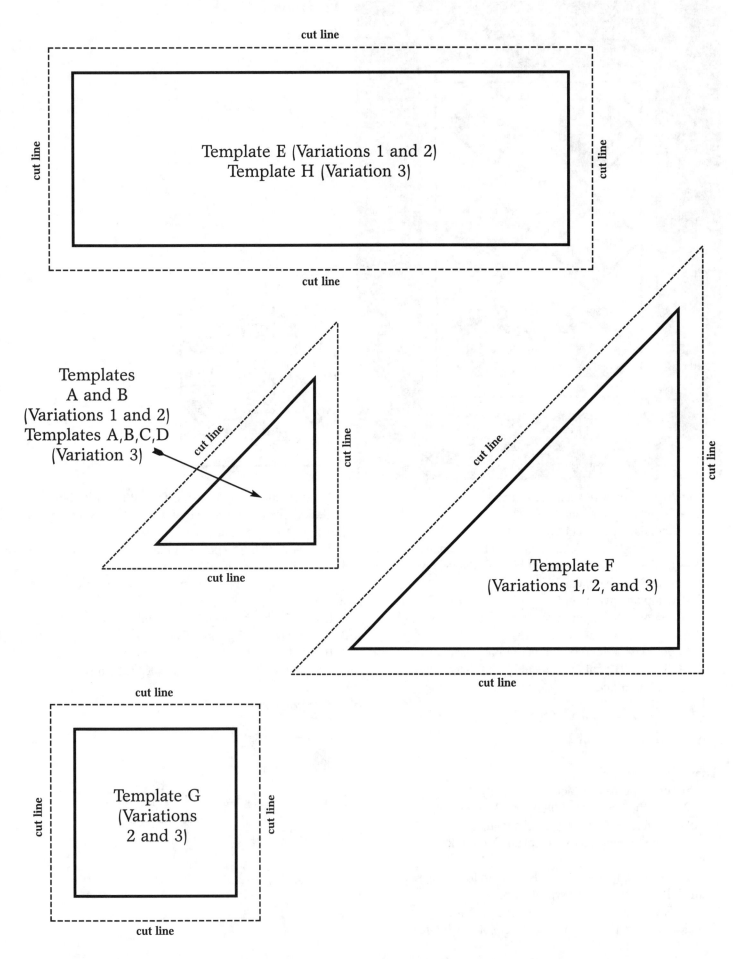

cut line

cut line

Template E (Variations 1 and 2)
Template H (Variation 3)

cut line

cut line

cut line

Templates
A and B
(Variations 1 and 2)
Templates A,B,C,D
(Variation 3)

cut line

cut line

cut line

cut line

cut line

Template F
(Variations 1, 2, and 3)

cut line

cut line

cut line

cut line

Template G
(Variations
2 and 3)

cut line

cut line

cut line

*45$\frac{1}{2}$" x 58$\frac{1}{8}$"*

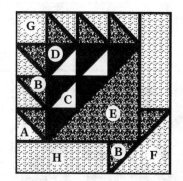

*Measurements given with seam allowances.*

A — Template given; cut 36
B — Template given; cut 48
C — Template given; cut 18
D — Template given; cut 36
E — 6$\frac{1}{4}$" x 6$\frac{1}{4}$"; cut 3; then cut in half diagonally
F — Template given; cut 6
G — Template given; cut 6
H — Template given; cut 12
I — 9$\frac{1}{2}$" x 9$\frac{1}{2}$"; cut 2
J — 9$\frac{7}{8}$" x 9$\frac{7}{8}$"; cut 3; then cut in half diagonally
K — 7$\frac{1}{4}$" x 7$\frac{1}{4}$"; cut 2; then cut in half diagonally
L — 2$\frac{1}{2}$" x 26"; cut 2
M — 2$\frac{1}{2}$" x 42$\frac{5}{8}$"; cut 2
N — 8$\frac{1}{2}$" x 30"; cut 2
O — 8$\frac{1}{2}$" x 58$\frac{5}{8}$", cut 2

## Assembly Instructions:

1. To form one Basket Block:

A. Sew the long side of Template A to the long side of Template B. Repeat 5 times (6 blocks total).

B. Sew the long side of Template C to the long side of Template D.

C. Sew together a horizontal strip of 4 pieces in the following order: Template G, B/A/ Unit, B/A Unit, B/A Unit.

D. Sew together a horizontal strip of 4 pieces in the following order: A/B Unit, D/C Unit, D/C Unit, Template D.

E. Sew together a horizontal strip of 3 pieces in the following order: B/A Unit, D/C Unit, Template D.

F. Sew together a horizontal strip of 2 pieces in the following order: A/B Unit, Template D.

G. Sew these four horizontal strips together to create a partial triangle.

H. Sew Template E onto pieced strips to create a block.

I. Sew one Template B to end of one Template H. Repeat (2 strips total).

2. Repeat 5 more times (6 blocks total).

3. See How to Assemble Your Quilt, Diagram 2, on page 10.

4. Follow Border Application Diagram on page 11 to complete your quilt, using Templates L through O.

## Fabric Requirements

□ — 1$\frac{1}{4}$ yds.

■ —$\frac{1}{4}$ yd.

▨ —3 yds.

▩ — 1 yd.

Backing — If using horizontal seams—3$\frac{1}{4}$ yds.
 If using vertical seams—2$\frac{1}{2}$ yds.
Batting— 48" x 61"

# Fan

*47" x 56"*

C. Sew Template J to pieced unit to create block.

D. Repeat 11 more times (12 blocks total).

3. See How to Assemble Your Quilt, Diagram 1, page 10.

4. Follow Border Application Diagram on page 11 to complete quilt, using Templates K through N.

*Measurements given with seam allowances.*

A — Template given; cut 12
B — Template given; cut 12
C — Template given; cut 12
D — Template given; cut 12
E — Template given; cut 12
F — Template given; cut 12
G — Template given; cut 12
H — Template given; cut 12
I — Template given; cut 12
J — Template given; cut 12
K — $2^1/2$" x $27^1/2$"; cut 2
L — $2^1/2$" x $40^1/2$"; cut 2
M — $8^1/2$" x $31^1/2$"; cut 2
N — $8^1/2$" x $56^1/2$"; cut 2

### Assembly Instructions:

1. To create one Fan Block:

A. Sew one Template B to one Template C. Sew Template D to B/C Unit. Continue sewing Templates E through I to Unit B/C/D.

B. Sew Template A to pieced unit.

## Fabric Requirements

— $7/8$ yd.

— $1/2$ yd.

— $1/8$ yd.

— $2^1/4$ yds.

— $1/4$ yd.

— $1/8$ yd.

— $3/8$ yd.

— $1/4$ yd.

— $3/8$ yd.

— $1/4$ yd.

Backing — If using horizontal seams—$3^1/8$ yds.
If using vertical seams—$2^5/8$ yds.

Batting— 50" x 59"

cut line

Template A (Variation 1)

Template C (Variation 2)

cut line

cut line

cut line

cut line

cut line

cut line

Templates
B through I
(Variation 1)

Templates
A and B
(Variation 2)

cut line

Template J (Variation 1)

Template D (Variation 2)

fold on dotted line

cut line

**Variation 2**

*47" x 56"*

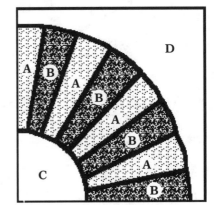

*Measurements given with seam allowances.*

A — Template given; cut 48
B — Template given; cut 48
C — Template given; cut 12
D — Template given; cut 12
E — 2½" x 27½"; cut 2
F — 2½" x 40½"; cut 2
G — 8½" x 31½"; cut 2
H — 8½" x 56½"; cut 2

### Assembly Instructions:

1. To create one Fan Block:

A. Sew one Template B to one Template A. Sew Template A to B/A Unit. Continue alternating Templates A and B to form the following: A/B/A/B/A/B/A/B.

B. Sew Template C to pieced unit.

C. Sew Template D to pieced unit to create block.

2. Repeat 11 more times (12 blocks total).

3. See How to Assemble Your Quilt, Diagram 1, page 10.

4. Follow Border Application Diagram on page 11 to complete quilt, using Templates E through H.

**Fabric Requirements**

☐ — 1⅛ yds.
▨ — 2⅞ yds.
▦ — 1⅛ yds.

Backing — If using horizontal seams—3⅛ yds.
If using vertical seams—2⅝ yds.
Batting— 49" x 57"

# Ocean Waves

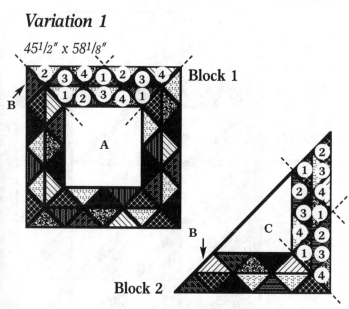

## Variation 1

45¹/₂" x 58¹/₈"

Block 1

Block 2

G. Repeat Steps A through F 6 times (7 blocks total).

2. To create one Ocean Wave Block 2:

A. Follow steps 1A and 1B, 6 times.

B. Sew a large triangle to 2 sides of Template C.

C. Repeat this step 9 more times (10 triangles total).

3. See How to Assemble Your Quilt, Diagram 2, page 10.

4. Follow Border Application Diagram on page 11 to complete your quilt, using Templates D through G.

*Measurements given with seam allowances.*

A — 5" x 5"; cut 7

B — Template given; cut 576 from 7 different fabrics

C — 5³/₈" x 5³/₈"; cut 5; then cut in half diagonally

D — 2¹/₂" x 26"; cut 2

E — 2¹/₂" x 42⁵/₈"; cut 2

F — 8¹/₂" x 30"; cut 2

G — 8¹/₂" x 58⁵/₈"; cut 2

## Assembly Instructions:

1. To create one Ocean Wave Block 1:

A. Create horizontal strip by sewing together 3 Template B's, following numbers 2 through 4.

B. Sew another Template B to the strip of 3 triangles, to create a large triangle.

C. Repeat entire process 11 more times (12 triangles total).

D. Sew a large triangle to top, bottom, and sides of Template A.

E. Sew together 2 large triangles (see step B) to form 1 larger triangle. Repeat 3 more times (4 larger triangles).

F. Sew a larger triangle to each side of the patch, to create a large block.

## Fabric Requirements

▮ — ³/₈ yd.

☐ — ⁵/₈ yd.

▨ — ³/₈ yd.

▥ — ³/₈ yd.

▩ — ³/₈ yd.

▧ — ³/₈ yd.

▦ — 2⁵/₈ yds.

▨ — ³/₈ yd.

Template B

cut line

cut line

cut line

Backing — If using horizontal seams—3¹/₄ yds.
If using vertical seams—2¹/₂ yds.

Batting— 49" x 61"

# Roman Stripe

## Variation 1

54 1/2" x 48"

*Measurements given with seam allowances.*

A — Template given; cut 20
B — Template given; cut 20
C — Template given; cut 20
D — Template given; cut 20
E — Template given; cut 20
F — 7 3/8" x 7 3/8"; cut 10; then cut in half diagonally
G — 3 1/2" x 26 1/2"; cut 2
H — 3 1/2" x 39; cut 2
I — 8 1/2" x 32 1/2" ; cut 2
J — 8 1/2" x 55"; cut 2

### Assembly Instructions:

1. To create one Roman Stripe Block:
   A. Sew Template A to Template B.
   B. Sew Template C to A/B Unit.
   C. Sew Template D to A/B/C Unit.
   D. Sew Template E to A/B/C/D Unit.
   E. Sew Template F to A/B/C/D/E Unit to create block.
   F. Repeat steps 1A through 1E 19 more times
(20 blocks total).

2. See How to Assemble Your Quilt, Diagram 1, page 10.

3. Follow Border Application Diagram on page 11 to complete your quilt, using Templates G through J.

### Fabric Requirements

— 7/8 yd.

— 7/8 yd.

— 1/8 yd.

— 2 1/8 yds.

— 1/2 yd.

— 3/4 yd.

Backing — If using horizontal seams—3 yds.
          If using vertical seams—2 5/8 yds.
Batting—58" x 51"

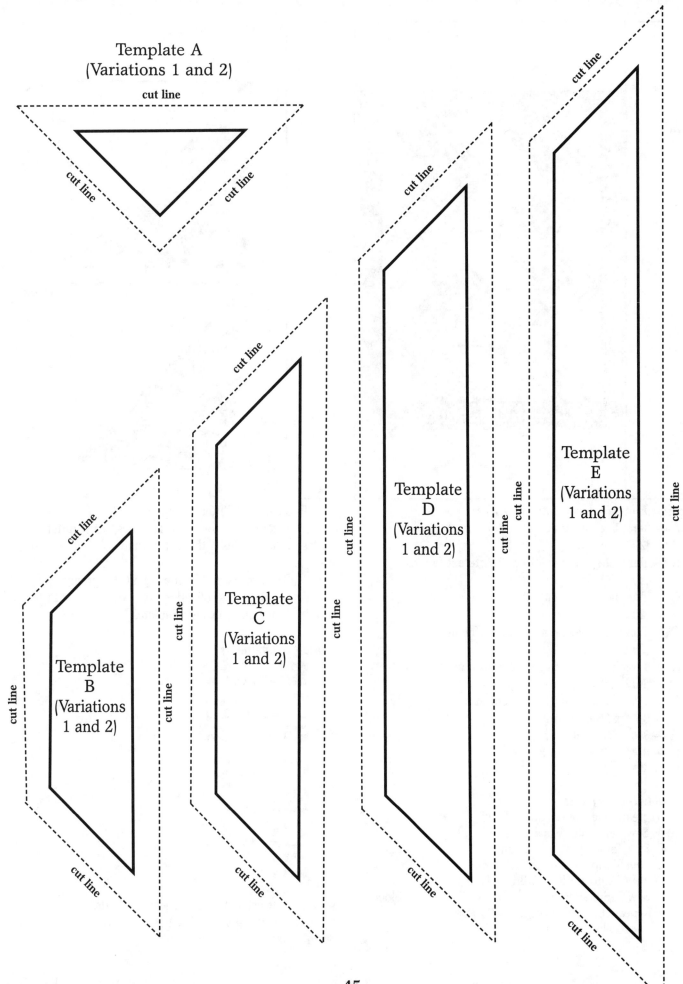

Template A
(Variations 1 and 2)

cut line

cut line

cut line

Template B
(Variations 1 and 2)

cut line

cut line

cut line

cut line

cut line

Template C
(Variations 1 and 2)

cut line

cut line

cut line

Template D
(Variations 1 and 2)

cut line

cut line

cut line

cut line

Template E
(Variations 1 and 2)

cut line

cut line

**Block 1**

**Block 2**

*Variation 2*

*54¹/₂" x 48"*

*Measurements given with seam allowances.*

A — Template given; cut 10 of 2 different fabrics (20 total)

B — Template given; cut 10 of 2 different fabrics (20 total)

C — Template given; cut 10 of 2 different fabrics (20 total)

D — Template given; cut 10 of 2 different fabrics (20 total)

E — Template given; cut 10 of 2 different fabrics (20 total)

F — 7³/₈" x 7³/₈"; cut 10; then cut in half diagonally

G — 3¹/₂" x 26¹/₂"; cut 2

H — 3¹/₂" x 39; cut 2

I — 8¹/₂" x 32¹/₂" ; cut 2

J — 8¹/₂" x 55"; cut 2

### Assembly Instructions:

1. To create one Roman Stripe Block 1:
   A. Sew Template A to Template B.
   B. Sew Template C to A/B Unit.
   C. Sew Template D to A/B/C Unit.
   D. Sew Template E to A/B/C/D Unit.
   E. Sew Template F to A/B/C/D/E Unit to create block.
   F. Repeat steps 1A through 1E 9 more times (10 blocks total).

2. To create one Roman Stripe Block 2:
   Repeat steps 1A through 1E 10 times, using different fabrics for Templates A through E than you used in Block 1.

3. See How to Assemble Your Quilt, Diagram 1, page 10.

4. Follow Border Application Diagram on page 11 to complete your quilt, using Templates G through J.

### Fabric Requirements

— ⁵/₈ yd.

— 2⁷/₈ yds.

— ¹/₂ yd.

— ³/₈ yd.

— ¹/₂ yd.

— ³/₈ yd.

— ¹/₄ yd.

Backing — If using horizontal seams—3 yds.
         If using vertical seams—2⁵/₈ yds.

Batting—58" x 51"

46

# Tumbling Blocks

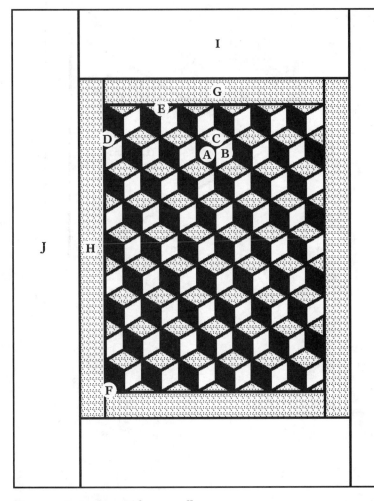

*48" x 55"*

*Measurements given with seam allowances.*

A — Template given; cut 54
B — Template given; cut 54
C — Template given; cut 44
D — Template given; cut 8
E — Template given; cut 11
F — Template given; cut 2
G — 3½" x 26½"; cut 2
H — 3½" x 39½" ; cut 2
I — 8½" x 32½"; cut 2
J — 8½" x 55½"; cut 2

### Assembly Instructions:

1. Sew one Template A to one Template B. Sew Template C to the top of A/B Unit. Repeat 43 more times (44 blocks total).

2. Sew one Template A to one Template B. Sew Template E to top of A/B Unit. Repeat 5 more times (6 blocks total).

3. Sew one Template B to one Template D. Repeat 3 more times (4 blocks total).

4. Sew one Template A to one Template D. Repeat 3 more times (4 blocks total).

5. Sew 5 A/B/C Units together to create a horizontal strip. Sew one D/B unit to left end of strip and one A/D unit to right. Repeat 3 times (4 horizontal strips.)

6. Sew 6 A/B/C Units together to create a horizontal strip. Repeat 3 times (4 horizontal total).

7. Sew 6 A/B/E Units together to create a horizontal strip.

8. Sew strip from step 7 to strip from Step 5. Add another strip from Step 6. Continue alternating strips from Step 5 and strips from Step 6, until all strips are used.

9. Sew the 2 Template F's and 5 Template E's along bottom of quilt.

10. Follow Border Application Diagram on page 11 to complete your quilt, using Templates G through J.

### Fabric Requirements

— ½ yd.

— 2⅝ yds.

— 1 yd.

Backing — If using horizontal seams—3 yds.
　　　　　If using vertical seams—2⅝ yds.
Batting—58" x 51"

# Bow Tie

## Variation 1

*45" x 55"*

**Fabric Requirements**

☐ — 1¹/₈ yds.

▨ — 2¹/₂ yds.

Backing — If using horizontal seams—3 yds.
If using vertical seams—2¹/₂ yds.
Batting— 48" x 58"

*Measurements given with seam allowances.*

A — 2¹/₄" x 2¹/₄"; cut 35
B — Template given; cut 140 (70 each of 2 fabrics)
C — 2¹/₂" x 25¹/₂"; cut 2
D — 2¹/₂" x 39¹/₂"; cut 2
E — 8¹/₂" x 29¹/₂"; cut 2
F — 8¹/₂" x 55¹/₂"; cut 2

## Assembly Instructions:

1. To create one Bow Tie Block:

A. Sew one Template B to one side of Template A.

B. Sew another Template B (of matching fabric to the first Template B) to the opposite side of Template A.

C. Sew a Template B of different fabric to each of the remaining sides of Template A.

D. Repeat 34 more times (35 blocks total).

2. See How to Assemble Your Quilt, Diagram 1, page 10.

3. Follow Border Application Diagram on page 11 to complete your quilt, using Templates C through F.

**Template B**
**(Variations 1, 2, and 3)**

cut line

## Variation 2

*45" x 55"*

*Measurements given with seam allowances.*

A — 2¼" x 2¼"; cut 18
B — Template given; cut 72 (36 each of 2 fabrics)
C — 5½" x 5½"; cut 17
D — 2½" x 25½"; cut 2
E — 2½" x 39½"; cut 2
F — 8½" x 29½"; cut 2
G — 8½" x 55½"; cut 2

### Fabric Requirements

■ — ¼ yd.
☐ — ⅝ yd.
▨ — 4 yds.

Backing — If using horizontal seams—3 yds.
If using vertical seams—2½ yds.
Batting— 48" x 58"

### Assembly Instructions:

1. To create one Bow Tie Block:

A. Sew one Template B to one side of Template A.

B. Sew another Template B (of matching fabric to the first Template B) to the opposite side of Template A.

C. Sew a Template B of different fabric to each of the remaining sides of Template A.

D. Repeat 17 more times (18 blocks total).

2. See How to Assemble Your Quilt, Diagram 1, page 10.

3. Follow Border Application Diagram on page 11 to complete your quilt, using Templates D through G.

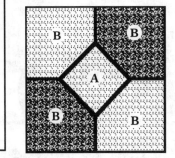

*Measurements given with seam allowances.*

    A — 2¹/₄" x 2¹/₄"; cut 20

    B — Template given; cut 80 (40 each of 2 fabrics)

    C — 4³/₈" x 4³/₈"; cut 2; then cut in half diagonally

    D — 5⁷/₈" x 5⁷/₈"; cut 7; then cut in half diagonally

    E — 5¹/₂" x 5¹/₂"; cut 12

    F — 2¹/₂" x 28³/₄; cut 2

    G — 2¹/₂" x 39¹/₂"; cut 2

    H — 8¹/₂" x 32³/₄"; cut 2

    I — 8¹/₂" x 55¹/₂"; cut 2

**Fabric Requirements**

☐ — 3 yds.

▧ — ¹/₂ yd.

▨ — ³/₄ yd.

Backing — If using horizontal seams—3¹/₈ yds.
             If using vertical seams—2⁵/₈ yds.

Batting— 51" x 58"

### Assembly Instructions:

    1. To create one Bow Tie Block:

        A. Sew one Template B to one side of Template A.

        B. Sew another Template B (of matching fabric to the first Template B) to the opposite side of Template A.

        C. Sew a Template B of different fabric to each of the remaining sides of Template A.

        D. Repeat 19 more times (20 blocks total).

    2. See How to Assemble Your Quilt, Diagram 2, page 10.

    3. Follow Border Application Diagram on page 11 to complete your quilt, using Templates F through I.

# Robbing Peter to Pay Paul

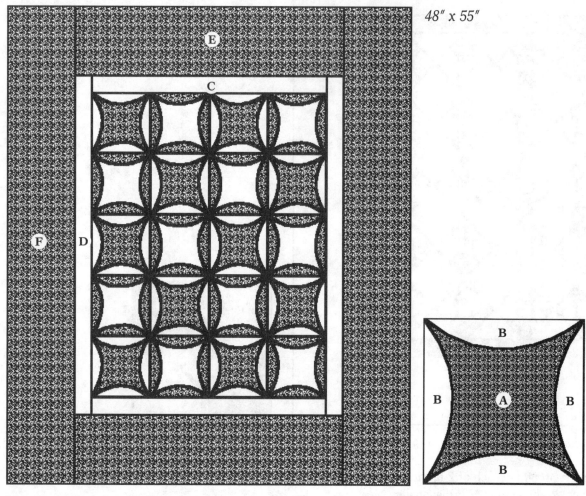

*48" x 55"*

*Measurements given with seam allowances.*
- A — Template given; cut 20 (10 each of 2 different fabrics)
- B — Template given; cut 80 (40 each of 2 different fabrics)
- C — 2$^{1/2}$" x 28$^{1/2}$"; cut 2
- D — 2$^{1/2}$" x 39$^{1/2}$"; cut 2
- E — 8$^{1/2}$" x 32$^{1/2}$"; cut 2
- F — 8$^{1/2}$" x 55$^{1/2}$"; cut 2

## Fabric Requirements

☐ — 1$^{1/4}$ yds.

▨ — 4$^{1/8}$ yds.

Backing — If using horizontal seams—3 yds.
              If using vertical seams—2$^{5/8}$ yds.
Batting— 51" x 58"

## Assembly Instructions:

1. To create one Robbing Peter to Pay Paul Block:
   A. Sew one Template B to one side of Template A.
   B. Sew another Template B to the opposite side of Template A.
   C. Sew another Template B to each of the remaining sides of Template A.
   D. Repeat 9 more times, always using matching fabrics for Template B and a contrasting fabric for Template A.
   E. Make 10 more blocks using Templates A and B, but reverse the fabrics used in Step D.
2. See How to Assemble Your Quilt, Diagram 1, page 10.
3. Follow Border Application Diagram on page 11 to complete your quilt, using Templates C through F.

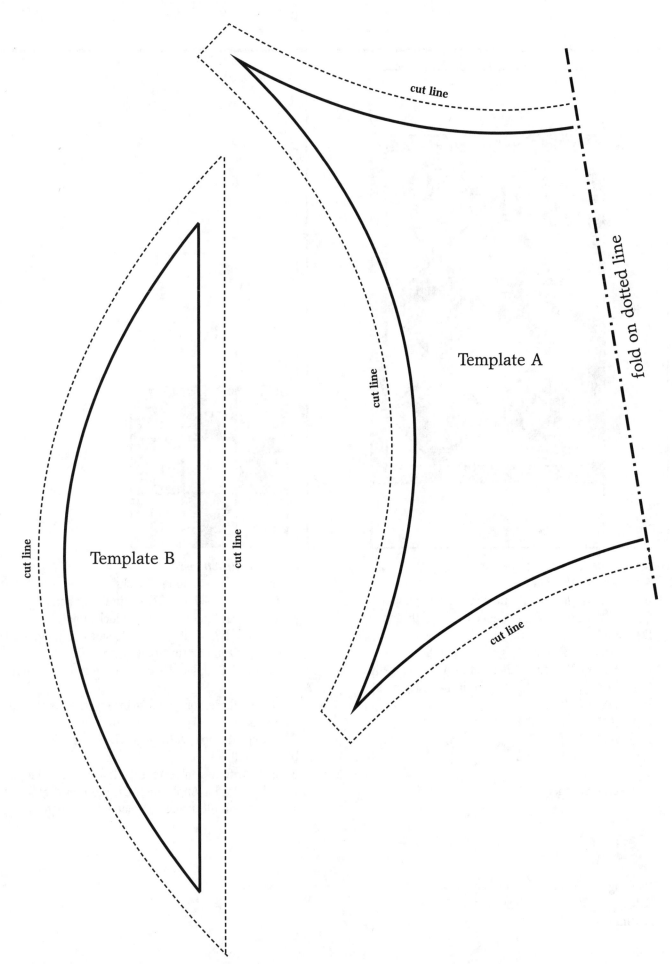

cut line

fold on dotted line

Template A

cut line

cut line

cut line

Template B

cut line

cut line

53

# Shoo-Fly

45 1/2" x 58 1/8"

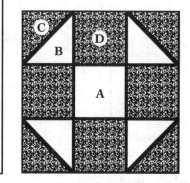

*Measurements given with seam allowances.*

A — 3 1/2" x 3 1/2"; cut 6
B — 3 7/8" x 3 7/8"; cut 12, then cut in half diagonally
C — 3 7/8" x 3 7/8"; cut 12, then cut in half diagonally
D — 3 1/2" x 3 1/2"; cut 24
E — 9 1/2" x 9 1/2"; cut 2
F — 9 7/8" x 9 7/8"; cut 3; then cut in half diagonally
G — 7 1/4" x 7 1/4"; cut 2; then cut in half diagonally
H — 2 1/2" x 26"; cut 2
I — 2 1/2" x 42 5/8"; cut 2
J — 8 1/2" x 30"; cut 2
K — 8 1/2" x 58 5/8", cut 2

## Fabric Requirements

☐ — 3 3/4 yds.

▨ — 1 1/8 yds.

Backing — If using horizontal seams—3 1/4 yds.
If using vertical seams—2 1/2 yds.
Batting— 48" x 61"

## Assembly Instructions:

1. To create one Shoo-Fly Block:

A. Sew long sides of Template B and Template C together. Repeat 3 more times (4 blocks total).

B. Sew a B/C Unit to opposite sides of Template D. Repeat (2 horizontal strips total).

C. Sew 2 Template Ds to opposite sides of a Template A.

D. Sew three horizontal strips together as shown on diagram above.

E. Repeat steps 1A through 1D 5 more times (6 blocks total).

3. See How to Assemble Your Quilt, Diagram 2, on page 10.

4. Follow Border Application Diagram on page 11 to complete your quilt, using Templates H through K.

# Crown of Thorns

45¹/₂" x 58¹/₈"

*Measurements given with seam allowances.*

A — Template given; cut 96
B — Template given; cut 96
C — Template given; cut 24
D — Template given; cut 30
E — 7¹/₄" x 7¹/₄"; cut 2; then cut in half diagonally
F — 9⁷/₈" x 9⁷/₈"; cut 3; then cut in half diagonally
G — 9¹/₂" x 9¹/₂"; cut 2
H — 2¹/₂" x 26"; cut 2
I — 2¹/₂" x 42⁵/₈"; cut 2
J — 8¹/₂" x 30¹/₂"; cut 2
K — 8¹/₂" x 58⁵/₈"; cut 2

## Assembly Instructions:

1. To create one Crown of Thorns Block:

A. Sew long side of Template A to long side of Template B. Repeat 15 more times (16 blocks total).

B. Sew together Row 1, working from left to right.

C. Sew together Row 2, working from left to right.

D. Repeat with 3 remaining rows.

E. Sew Row 1 to Row 2.

F. Sew Row 3 to other side of Row 2.

G. Repeat with remaining rows.

H. Repeat Steps 1A through Step 1G 5 more times (6 blocks total).

2. See How to Assemble Your Quilt, Diagram 2, on page 10.

3. Follow Border Application Diagram on page 11 to complete your quilt, using Templates H through K.

## Fabric Requirements

☐ — 3⁷/₈ yds.

▨ — 1 yd.

Backing — If using horizontal seams—3¹/₄ yds.
If using vertical seams—2¹/₂ yds.
Batting— 48" x 61"

# Monkey Wrench

56

## Variation 1

*43³/4" x 56"*

Measurements given with seam allowances.

A — Template given; cut 30
B — Template given; cut 24
C — Template given; cut 24
D — Template given; cut 24
E — 9¹/2" x 3³/4"; cut 8
F — 3³/4" x 40¹/2"; cut 3
G — 8¹/2" x 28¹/4"; cut 2
H — 8¹/2" x 56¹/2"; cut 2

### Fabric Requirements

— 1¹/8 yds.

— ¹/2 yd.

— ¹/2 yd.

Backing — If using horizontal seams—1¹/2 yds.
   If using vertical seams—2³/8 yds.
Batting— 47" x 59"

### Assembly Instructions:

1. To create one Monkey Wrench Block:
   A. Sew long sides of Template C and Template D together. Repeat 3 more times (4 blocks total).
   B. Sew a Template A to a Template B. Repeat (2 strips).
   C. Sew two C/D Units to opposite sides of an A/B Unit. (See diagram above.) Make a second such strip.
   D. Sew a template A to a Template B. Sew a Template A to the A/B Unit. Sew a Template B to the A/B/A Unit. Sew a Template A to the A/B/A/B Unit.
   E. Sew the three strips together as shown on diagram to create block.
   F. Repeat steps 1A through 1E, 5 more times (6 blocks total).

2. Sew a Template E to top of a block. Repeat 5 more times (6 blocks total).

3. Sew together 3 blocks to create vertical strip. Repeat (2 strips total).

4. Sew a Template E to the bottom of each vertical strip.

5. Sew a Template F to the left of each strip.

6. Sew strips together. Sew a Template F to the right of the final block.

7. Follow Border Application Diagram on page 11 to complete your quilt, using Templates G and H.

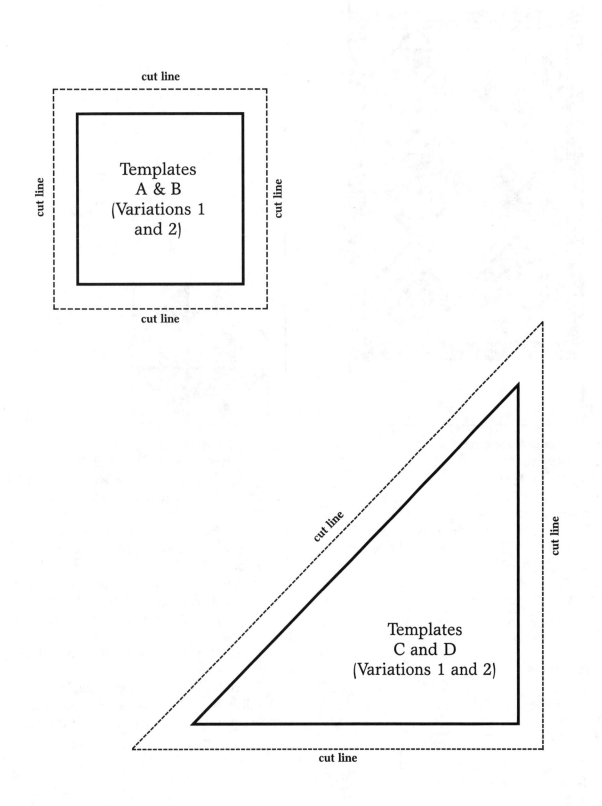

cut line

cut line

cut line

cut line

Templates
A & B
(Variations 1
and 2)

cut line

cut line

Templates
C and D
(Variations 1 and 2)

cut line

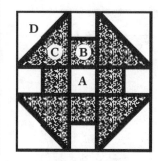

## Variation 2

*45¹/₂" x 58¹/₈"*

*Measurements given with seam allowances.*

A — Template given; cut 30
B — Template given; cut 24
C — Template given; cut 24
D — Template given; cut 24
E — 7¹/₄" x 7¹/₄"; cut 2; then cut in half diagonally
F — 9⁷/₈" x 9⁷/₈"; cut 3; then cut in half diagonally
G — 9¹/₂" x 9¹/₂"; cut 2
H — 2¹/₂" x 26"; cut 2
I — 2¹/₂" x 42⁵/₈"; cut 2
J — 8¹/₂" x 30"; cut 2
K — 8¹/₂" x 58⁵/₈"; cut 2

### Fabric Requirements

☐ — 3³/₄ yds.

▓ — ³/₄ yd.

Backing — If using horizontal seams—3¹/₄ yds.
　　　　　If using vertical seams—2¹/₂ yds.
Batting— 48" x 61"

### Assembly Instructions:

1. To create one Monkey Wrench Block:

A. Sew long sides of Template C and Template D together. Repeat 3 more times (4 blocks total).

B. Sew a Template A to a Template B. Repeat (2 strips).

C. Sew two C/D Units to opposite sides of an A/B Unit. (See diagram above.) Make a second such strip.

D. Sew a template A to a Template B. Sew a Template A to the A/B Unit. Sew a Template B to the A/B/A Unit. Sew a Template A to the A/B/A/B Unit.

E. Sew the three strips together as shown on diagram to create block.

F. Repeat steps 1A through 1E, 5 more times (6 blocks total).

2. See How to Assemble Your Quilt, Diagram 2, page 10.

3. Follow Border Application Diagram on page 11 to complete your quilt, using Templates H through K.

# Carolina Lily

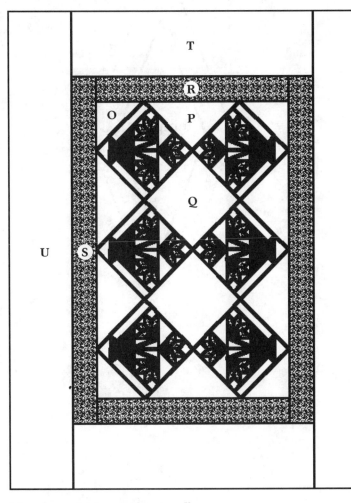

45½" x 58⅛"

*Measurements given with seam allowances.*

A — Template given; cut 72
B — 2⅝" x 2⅝"; cut 9, then cut in half diagonally
C — 2⅛" x 2⅛"; cut 6, then cut in half diagonally
D — 1¾" x 1¾"; cut 6
E — 1¾" x 1¾"; cut 12
F — 2⅛" x 2⅛"; cut 6; then cut in half diagonally
G — 2⅛" x 2⅛"; cut 6; then cut in half diagonally
H — 3⅞" x 3⅞"; cut 6; then cut in half diagonally
I — 3" x 3½"; cut 6
J — 5⅛" x 5⅛"; cut 3; then cut in half diagonally
K — 6½" x 1¾"; cut 12
L — 2⅛" x 2⅛"; cut 6; then cut in half diagonally
M — 3⅜" x 3⅜"; cut 3; then cut in half diagonally
N — ¾" x 3¾"; cut 18
O — 6⅞" x 6⅞"; cut 2; then cut in half diagonally
P — 9⅜" x 9⅜"; cut 3; then cut in half diagonally
Q — 9" x 9"; cut 2
R — 3½" x 24½"; cut 2
S — 3½" x 42½"; cut 2
T — 8½" x 30½"; cut 2
U — 8½" x 58½", cut 2

## Fabric Requirements

Backing — If using horizontal seams—3¼ yds.
              If using vertical seams—2½ yds.
Batting— 49" x 61"

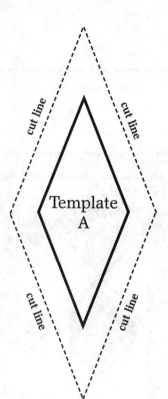

*Assembly Instructions:*

1. To create one Carolina Lily Block:

    A. Sew together 4 Template A's.

    B. Insert 2 Template C's and 1 Template D into top of A/A/A/A unit.

    C. Sew Template B to the bottom of unit to form a square.

    D. Sew a Template H to A/B side of square. Sew another Template H to B/A side of square. (Unit 1)

    E. Sew together 4 Template A's. Repeat.

    F. Insert a Template E into one corner of A/A/A/A unit. Insert a Template E into the opposite corner of the second A/A/A/A unit.

    G. Insert a Template F into the top center of each of those units.

    H. Insert a Template G into the remaining corner of each of those units.

    I. Sew a Template B to the bottom of both units.

    J. Sew Template I between the two units to create horizontal strip. (Unit 2)

    K. Sew bottom of Unit 1 to top of Unit 2. (Unit 3)

    L. Sew Template J to bottom of Unit 3. (Unit 4)

    M. Sew Template L to Template K. Repeat.

    N. Sew L/K to lower left side of Unit 4. Sew second L/K to lower right side of Unit 4. (Unit 5)

    O. Sew Template M to bottom of Unit 5.

    P. Fold under edges of 3 Templates N and slipstitch into position as shown on diagram. Adjust lengths as needed.

    Q. Repeat steps 1A through 1P 5 more times (6 blocks total).

  2. See How to Assemble Your Quilt, Diagram 2, page 10.

  3. Follow Border Application Diagram on page 11 to complete your quilt, using Templates R through U.

# Bear Paw

*45¹/₂" x 58¹/₈"*

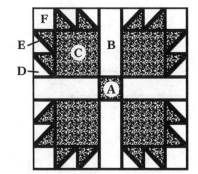

*Measurements given with seam allowances.*

A — Template given; cut 6
B — Template given; cut 24
C — Template given; cut 24
D — Template given; cut 96
E — Template given; cut 96
F — Template given; cut 24
G — 7¹/₄" x 7¹/₄"; cut 2; then cut in half diagonally
H — 9⁷/₈" x 9⁷/₈"; cut 3; then cut in half diagonally
I — 9¹/₂" x 9¹/₂"; cut 2
J — 2¹/₂" x 26"; cut 2
K — 2¹/₂" x 42⁵/₈"; cut 2
L — 8¹/₂" x 30"; cut 2
M — 8¹/₂" x 58⁵/₈"; cut 2

## Fabric Requirements

⬜ — 5⁵/₈ yds.

▨ — 1¹/₄ yds.

Backing — If using horizontal seams—3¹/₂ yds.
           If using vertical seams—2¹/₂ yds.
Batting— 48" x 61"

## Assembly Instructions:

1. To create one Bear Paw Block:

A. Sew long sides of Template D and Template E together. Repeat 15 more times (16 blocks total).

B. Sew a D/E unit to another D/E unit. (See diagram.) Repeat 7 more times (8 strips total).

C. Sew a Template C to a D/E strip. Repeat 3 more times (4 blocks total).

D. Sew a Template F to end of a D/E strip. Repeat s3 more times (4 strips total).

E. Sew D/E/F strip to C/D/E strip to create block. Repeat 3 more times (4 blocks total) to create Unit 1.

F. Sew a Unit 1 to the long side of a Template B. Sew another Unit 1 to the other long side of the same Template B. Repeat. (2 strips total.)

G. Sew Template A to the short end of a Template B. Sew the short end of another Template B to the opposite side of the same Template A.

H. Sew three strips together as shown on diagram.

I. Repeat steps 1A through 1 H 5 more times (6 blocks total).

2. See How to Assemble Your Quilt, **Diagram 2**, on page 10.

3. Follow Border Application **Diagram on page 11** to complete your quilt, using Templates J through M.

cut line

Templates
A & F

cut line

cut line

cut line

cut line

Template B

cut line

cut line

cut line

cut line

Template C

cut line

cut line

cut line

cut line

cut line

Templates
D & E

cut line

# Pinwheel

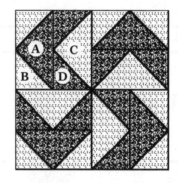

*Measurements given with seam allowances.*
- A — Template given; cut 24
- B — 3¹/₈″ x 3¹/₈″; cut 24; then cut in half diagonally
- C — Template given; cut 24
- D — 3¹/₈″ x 3¹/₈″; cut 24; then cut in half diagonally
- E — 7¹/₄″ x 7¹/₄″; cut 2; then cut in half diagonally
- F — 9⁷/₈″ x 9⁷/₈″; cut 3; then cut in half diagonally
- G — 9¹/₂″ x 9¹/₂″; cut 2
- H — 2¹/₂″ x 26″; cut 2
- I — 2¹/₂″ x 42⁵/₈″; cut 2
- J — 8¹/₂″ x 30″; cut 2
- K — 8¹/₂″ x 58⁵/₈″; cut 2

### Assembly Instructions:

1. To create one Pinwheel Block:

A. Sew Template B to Template A. (See diagram.) Sew another Template B to the other side of Template A. Repeat 3 times (4 strips total).

B. Sew Template D to Template C. (See diagram.) Sew another Template D to the other side of Template C. Repeat 3 times (4 strips total).

C. Sew A/B unit to C/D unit. (See diagram.) Repeat 3 times (4 blocks total).

D. Sew 4 blocks together as shown to create large block.

E. Repeat steps 1A through 1D 5 more times (6 blocks total).

2. See How to Assemble Your Quilt, Diagram 2, on page 10.

3. Follow Border Application Diagram on page 11 to complete your quilt, using Templates H through K.

### Fabric Requirements

— 1¹/₈ yds.

— 2³/₄ yds.

— 1 yd.

Backing — If using horizontal seams—3¹/₄ yds.
If using vertical seams—2¹/₂ yds.
Batting— 48″ x 61″

Templates
A & C
(Variation 1)

Template A
(Variation 2)

Template B
(Variation 3)

cut line

cut line

cut line

cut line

cut line

cut line

Template A (Variation 3)

cut line

*Measurements given with seam allowances.*

A — Template given; cut 24
B — 3¹/₈″ x 3¹/₈″; cut 24; then cut in half diagonally
C — 2³/₄″ x 5″; cut 24
D — 7¹/₄″ x 7¹/₄″; cut 2; then cut in half diagonally
E — 9⁷/₈″ x 9⁷/₈″; cut 3; then cut in half diagonally
F — 9¹/₂″ x 9¹/₂″; cut 2
G — 2¹/₂″ x 26″; cut 2
H — 2¹/₂″ x 42⁵/₈″; cut 2
I— 8¹/₂″ x 30″; cut 2
J — 8¹/₂″ x 58⁵/₈″; cut 2

### Assembly Instructions:

1. To create one Pinwheel Block:

A. Sew Template B to Template A. (See diagram.) Sew another Template B to the other side of Template A. Repeat 3 times (4 strips total).

B. Sew Template C to B/A/B unit. Repeat 3 times (24 blocks total).

C. Sew 4 blocks together as shown to create large block.

D. Repeat steps 1A through 1C 5 more times (6 blocks total).

2. See How to Assemble Your Quilt, Diagram 2, on page 10.

3. Follow Border Application Diagram on page 11 to complete your quilt, using Templates G through J.

### Fabric Requirements

■ — ⁵/₈ yd.

□ — 1¹/₈ yds.

▨ — 2³/₈ yds.

▓ — ¹/₂ yd.

Backing — If using horizontal seams—3¹/₄ yds.
If using vertical seams—2¹/₂ yds.

Batting— 48″ x 61″

## Variation 3

*45¹/₂" x 58¹/₈"*

*Measurements given with seam allowances.*

A — Template given; cut 24
B — Template given; cut 24
C — 7¹/₄" x 7¹/₄"; cut 2; then cut in half diagonally
D — 9⁷/₈" x 9⁷/₈"; cut 3; then cut in half diagonally
E — 9¹/₂" x 9¹/₂"; cut 2
F — 2¹/₂" x 26"; cut 2
G — 2¹/₂" x 42⁵/₈"; cut 2
H— 8¹/₂" x 30"; cut 2
I— 8¹/₂" x 58⁵/₈"; cut 2

### Fabric Requirements

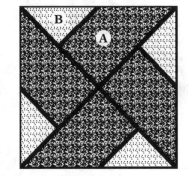

☐ — 1¹/₈ yds.

▦ — 2³/₈ yds.

▨ — 3/4 yd.

Backing — If using horizontal seams—3¹/₄ yds.
          If using vertical seams—2¹/₂ yds.
Batting— 48" x 61"

### Assembly Instructions:

1. To create one Pinwheel Block:

   A. Sew Template B to Template A. (See diagram.)
Repeat 3 times (4 triangles total).

   B. Sew unit B/A to unit B/A. (See diagram.) Repeat.
(Unit 1)

   C. Sew Unit 1 to Unit 1 to create block as shown.

   D. Repeat steps 1A through 1C 5 more times (6
blocks total).

2. See How to Assemble Your Quilt, Diagram 2, on page 10.

3. Follow Border Application Diagram on page 11 to
complete your quilt, using Templates F through I.

# Garden Maze

*48¹/₄" x 60"*

Measurements given with seam allowances.

A — Template given; cut 12
B — Template given; cut 48
C — Template given; cut 48
D — Template given; cut 34
E — 2⁷/₈" x 7¹/₂"; cut 17
F — 7¹/₂" x 7¹/₂"; cut 6
G — 2¹/₂" x 28³/₄"; cut 2
H — 2¹/₂" x 44¹/₂"; cut 2
I — 8¹/₂" x 32³/₄"; cut 2
J — 8¹/₂" x 60¹/₂"; cut 2

## Fabric Requirements

☐ — 3³/₈ yds.

▨ — 2⁵/₈ yds.

Backing — If using horizontal seams— 3³/₈ yds.
          If using vertical seams—2⁵/₈ yds.
Batting— 51" x 63"

## Assembly Instructions:

1. To create one Garden Maze Block:
  A. Sew Template C to Template B. Sew another Template C to opposite side of Template B. Repeat.
  B. Sew Template A to one end of Template B. Sew another Template B to opposite side of Template A.
  C. Sew together those 3 units, as shown on diagram, to create block.
  D. Repeat steps 1A through 1C 11 more times (12 blocks total).

2. To create one Garden Maze Strip:
  A. Sew long side of a Template D to long side of a Template E. Sew another Template D to opposite side of Template E.
  B. Repeat 16 more times (17 strips total).

3. Sew an A/B/C block to each short end of a D/E strip. Add another D/E strip and an A/B/C block. Repeat 3 more times (4 strips total).

4. Sew a D/E strip to one end of an F block. Sew another D/E strip to the opposite end of the F block. Create a horizontal strip by adding another F block and another D/E strip. Repeat 2 more times (3 strips total).

5. Sew strips together from top to bottom as shown on diagram.

6. See How to Assemble Your Quilt, Diagram 1, on page 10.

7. Follow Border Application Diagram on page 11 to complete your quilt, using Templates G through J.

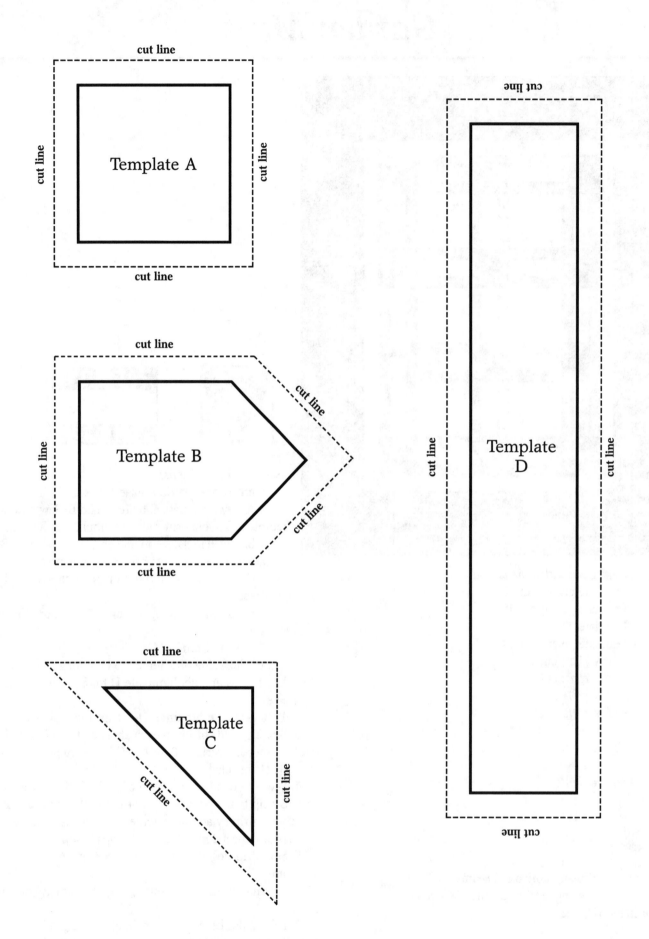

cut line

cut line

cut line

cut line

Template A

cut line

cut line

cut line

cut line

cut line

Template B

cut line

cut line

cut line

Template
C

cut line

cut line

cut line

cut line

Template
D

cut line

cut line

cut line

# Railroad Crossing

50" x 65"

*Measurements given with seam allowances.*

A — 7$\frac{1}{2}$" x 7$\frac{1}{2}$"; cut 8
B — Template given; cut 24
C — Template given; cut 48
D — Template given; cut 48
E — Template given; cut 48
F — Template given; cut 48
G — 5$\frac{1}{2}$" x 5$\frac{1}{2}$"; cut 4
H — 4$\frac{3}{8}$" x 4$\frac{3}{8}$"; cut 5; then cut in half diagonally
I — 7$\frac{7}{8}$" x 7$\frac{7}{8}$"; cut 3; then cut in half diagonally
J — 4" x 4"; cut 7
K — 2$\frac{1}{2}$" x 30$\frac{1}{2}$"; cut 2
L — 2$\frac{1}{2}$" x 49$\frac{1}{2}$"; cut 2
M — 8$\frac{1}{2}$" x 34$\frac{1}{2}$"; cut 2
N — 8$\frac{1}{2}$" x 65$\frac{1}{2}$"; cut 2

## Assembly Instructions:

1. To create one Railroad Crossing Strip:
   A. Sew Template F to Template E.
   B. Sew Template D to F/E Unit.
   C. Continue adding pieces so that final strip is F/E/D/C/B/C/D/E/F.

D. Repeat 23 more times (24 strips total).

2. See How to Assemble Your Quilt, Diagram 1, page 10.

3. Follow Border Application Diagram on page 11 to complete your quilt, using Templates K through N.

## Fabric Requirements

— $\frac{1}{2}$ yd.

— 2$\frac{1}{4}$ yds.

— $\frac{1}{2}$ yd.

— $\frac{1}{2}$ yd.

— $\frac{1}{2}$ yd.

— 3$\frac{1}{2}$ yds.

Backing — If using horizontal seams—3$\frac{5}{8}$ yds.
          If using vertical seams—2$\frac{3}{4}$ yds.
Batting— 53" x 68"

# Double Wedding Ring

*44" x 56"*

Measurements given with seam allowances.

- A — Template given; cut 24
- B — Template given; cut 48
- C — Template given; cut 48
- D — Template given; cut 48
- E — Template given; cut 48
- F — Template given; cut 48
- G — Template given; cut 24
- H — Template given; cut 24
- I — Template given; cut 8
- J — Template given; cut 6
- K — Template given; cut 4
- L — 2$\frac{1}{2}$" x 24$\frac{1}{2}$"; cut 2
- M — 2$\frac{1}{2}$" x 40$\frac{1}{2}$"; cut 2
- N — 8$\frac{1}{2}$" x 28$\frac{1}{2}$"; cut 2
- O — 8$\frac{1}{2}$" x 56$\frac{1}{2}$"; cut 2

**Fabric Requirements**

- ☐ — 3$\frac{1}{2}$ yds.
- ▦ — $\frac{1}{2}$ yd.
- ▦ — $\frac{5}{8}$ yd.
- ▨ — $\frac{1}{8}$ yd.
- ▦ — $\frac{1}{8}$ yd.
- ▦ — $\frac{1}{4}$ yd.

Backing — If using horizontal seams—1$\frac{1}{2}$ yd
           If using vertical seams—2$\frac{1}{2}$ yds.

Batting— 47" x 59"

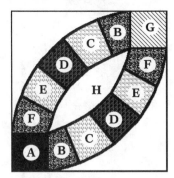

**Assembly Instructions:**

1. To create one Double Wedding Ring:
   A. Sew Template C to Template B.
   B. Sew Template D to B/C Unit.
   C. Sew Template E to B/C/D Unit.
   D. Sew Template F to B/C/D/E Unit (Strip 1).
   E. Sew Template H to inside of Strip 1 (Strip 2).
   F. Sew Template F to Template A.
   G. Sew Template E to A/F Unit.
   H. Sew Template D to A/F/E Unit.
   I. Sew Template C to A/F/E/D Unit.
   J. Sew Template B to A/F/E/D/C Unit.
   K. Sew Template G to A/F/E/D/C/B Unit (Strip 3).
   L. Sew Strip 3 to Strip 2 to create oval.
   M. Repeat 23 times (24 ovals total).

2. Sew oval to one side of Template I. Sew a second oval to the top of Template I. Repeat 7 times (8 partial blocks total).

3. Sew 2 blocks together to make strip. Repeat 2 times (3 strips total).

4. Sew an oval to top right corner of Template J. Sew to left side of partial block.

5. Sew an oval to top right corner of another Template J. Sew to right side of partial block.

6. Sew blocks from Steps 4 and 5 together.

7. Repeat steps 4 through 6.

8. Sew Strip of 2 blocks to Strip of 1 block.

9. Add Strip of 2 blocks.

10. Add Strip of 1 block.

11. Add Strip of 2 blocks.

12. Sew a Template K to an oval. Repeat.

13. Sew two ovals to Template J.

14. Sew Template K oval to Template J oval. Add a Template J Oval.

15. Sew a Template K in each of the top corners.

16. Sew a Template J at the top of the quilt and 2 Template J's to each side.

17. Follow Border Application Diagram on page 11 to complete your quilt, using Templates L through O.

71

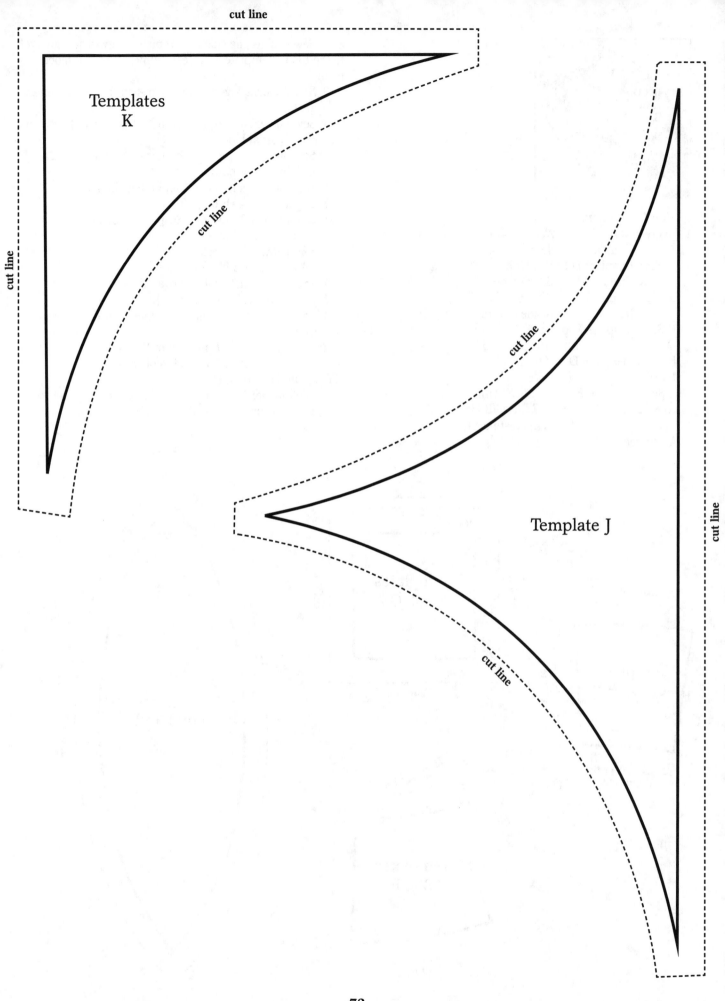

cut line

Templates
K

cut line

cut line

cut line

Template J

cut line

cut line

72

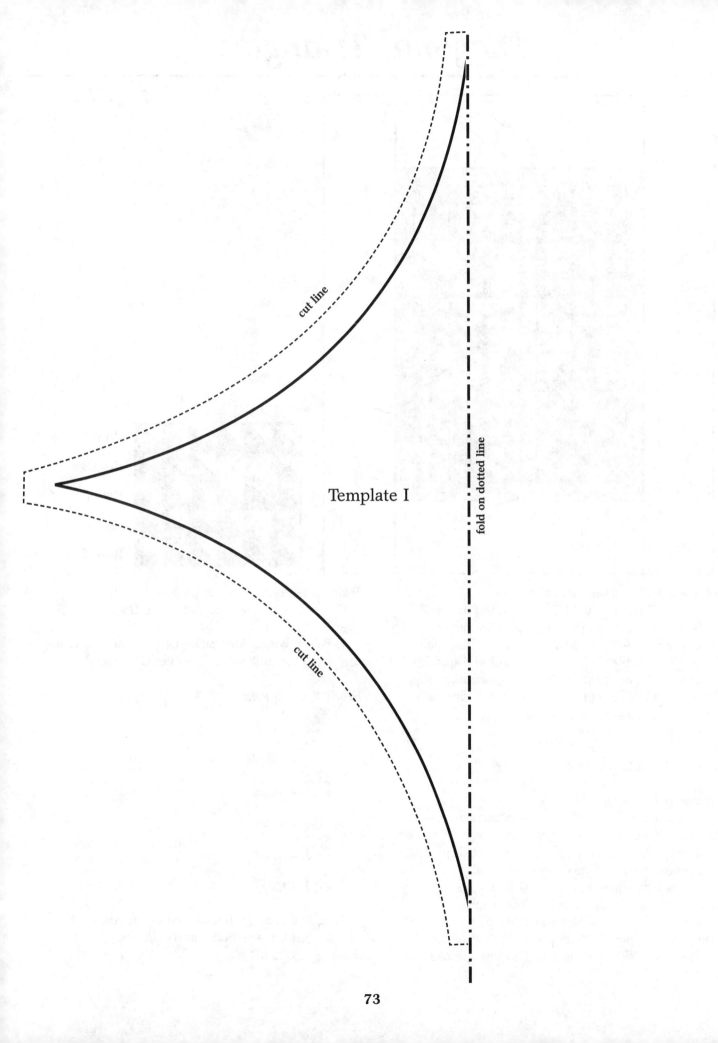

cut line

Template I

fold on dotted line

cut line

# Diagonal Triangles

*44" x 52"*

| | A | C | D | E | F | | |
|---|---|---|---|---|---|---|---|
| | | | | | | B | Row 1 |
| | | | | | | | Row 2 |
| | | | | | | | Row 3 |
| | | | | | | | Row 4 |
| | | | | | | | Row 5 |

*Measurements given with seam allowances.*

A — 2⁷⁄₈" x 2⁷⁄₈"; cut 20; then cut in half diagonally
B — 2⁷⁄₈" x 2⁷⁄₈"; cut 96; then cut in half diagonally
C — 2⁷⁄₈" x 2⁷⁄₈"; cut 20; then cut in half diagonally
D — 2⁷⁄₈" x 2⁷⁄₈"; cut 19; then cut in half diagonally
E — 2⁷⁄₈" x 2⁷⁄₈"; cut 19; then cut in half diagonally
F — 2⁷⁄₈" x 2⁷⁄₈"; cut 19; then cut in half diagonally
G — 2¹⁄₂" x 24¹⁄₂"; cut 2
H — 2¹⁄₂" x 36¹⁄₂"; cut 2
I — 8¹⁄₂" x 28¹⁄₂"; cut 2
J — 8¹⁄₂" x 52¹⁄₂"; cut 2

## Assembly Instructions:

1. Sew long side of a Template A to long side of a Template B. Repeat 38 times (39 blocks total).

2. Sew long side of a Template C to long side of a Template B. Repeat 38 times (39 blocks total).

3. Sew long side of a Template D to long side of a Template B. Repeat 37 times (38 blocks total).

4. Sew long side of a Template E to long side of a Template B. Repeat 37 times (38 blocks total).

5. Sew long side of a Template F to long side of a Template B. Repeat 37 times (38 blocks total).

6. See How to Assemble Your Quilt, Diagram 1, page 10.

7. Follow Border Application Diagram on page 11 to complete your quilt, using Templates G through J.

## Fabric Requirements

- ⬛ — ⁷⁄₈ yd.
- ⬜ — 2¹⁄₄ yds.
- ▦ — ¹⁄₂ yd.
- ▒ — ¹⁄₄ yd.
- ▨ — ¹⁄₄ yd.
- ⬚ — ¹⁄₄ yd.

Backing — If using horizontal seams—1¹⁄₂ yds.
If using vertical seams—2¹⁄₂ yds.
Batting— 49" x 57"

# Drunkard's Path

*48" x 62"*

Measurements given with seam allowances.
- A — Template given; cut 48
- B — Template given; cut 48
- C — Template given; cut 48
- D — Template given; cut 48
- E — 2½" x 28½"; cut 2
- F — 2½" x 46½"; cut 2
- G — 8½" x 32½"; cut 2
- H — 8½" x 62½"; cut 2

## Fabric Requirements

— 1⅛ yds.

— ½ yd.

Backing — If using horizontal seams—3½ yds.
If using vertical seams—2⅝ yds.
Batting— 53" x 67"

## Assembly Instructions:

1. To create one Drunkard's Path Block:

A. Sew curved side of Template A to curved side of Template B. Repeat 7 more times (8 blocks total).

B. Sew curved side of Template C to curved side of Template D. Repeat 7 more times (8 blocks total).

C. Sew together Row 1, working from left to right.

D. Repeat process with Rows 2, 3, and 4.

E. Sew Row 1 to Row 2.

F. Sew Row 3 to Row 2.

G. Sew Row 4 to Row 3 to create block.

H. Repeat steps 1A through 1G 5 more times (6 blocks total).

2. See How to Assemble Your Quilt, Diagram 1, page 10.

3. Follow Border Application Diagram on page 11 to complete your quilt, using Templates E through H.

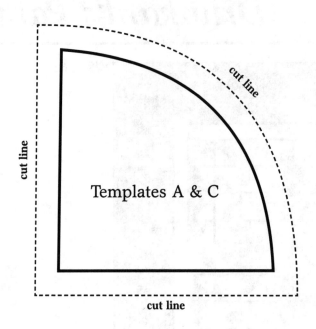

cut line

cut line

Templates A & C

cut line

cut line

cut line

cut line

Templates B & D

cut line

cut line

# Tree of Life

45¹/₂″ x 58¹/₂″

Template D

Templates A
& B

## Fabric Requirements

☐ — 1¹/₈ yds.

▨ — ¹/₂ yd.

▨ — ¹/₂ yd.

Backing — If using horizontal seams—3¹/₄ yds.
    If using vertical seams—2¹/₂ yds.
Batting— 50″ x 63″

*Measurements given with seam allowances.*

A — Template given; cut 6
B — Template given; cut 6
C — Template given; cut 12
D — Template given; cut 12
E — Template given; cut 6
F — Template given; cut 12
G — Template given; cut 150
H — Template given; cut 150
I — Template given; cut 12

J — 9¹/₂″ x 9¹/₂″; cut 2
K — 9⁷/₈″ x 9⁷/₈″; cut 3; then cut in half diagonally
L — 7¹/₄″ x 7¹/₄″; cut 2; then cut in half diagonally
M — 2¹/₂″ x 26; cut 2
N — 2¹/₂″ x 42⁵/₈; cut 2
O — 8¹/₂″ x 30; cut 2
P — 8¹/₂″ x 58⁵/₈; cut 2

77

## Assembly Instructions:

1. To create one Tree of Life Block:

A. Sew long side of Template A to long side of Template B.

B. Sew Template C to Template D. Repeat.

C. Sew A/B Block to C/D Block.

D. Sew Template E to another C/D Block.

E. Sew strip A/B/C/D to strip C/D/E.

F. Sew long side of Template H to long side of Template G. Repeat 18 more times (19 blocks total).

G. Sew together Row 1, working from left to right, ignoring Template I.

H. Sew together Row 2, working from left to right, ignoring Template I.

I. Sew together Row 3, working from left to right, ignoring Template I.

J. Sew Row 1 to Row 2 (Unit 1).

K. Sew Row 3 to Row 2 (Unit 2).

L. Sew Template I to Unit 2.

M. Sew three G/H Blocks together (Unit 3).

N. Sew two G/H Blocks together (Unit 4).

O. Sew Template G to Unit 4 (Unit 5).

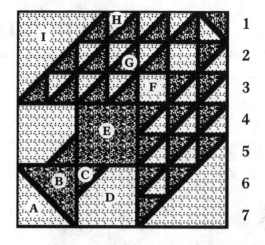

P. Sew Template G to a G/H Block (Unit 6).

Q. Sew Unit 3 to Unit 5. Sew Unit 6 to Unit 5 (Unit 7). Sew Template G to bottom of Unit 7 (Unit 8).

R. Sew Unit 8 to block A/B/C/D/E.

S. Repeat steps 1A though 1R 5 more times (6 blocks total).

2. See How to Assemble Your Quilt, Diagram 2, page 10.

3. Follow Border Application Diagram on page 11 to complete your quilt, using Templates M through P.

# Bachelor's Puzzle

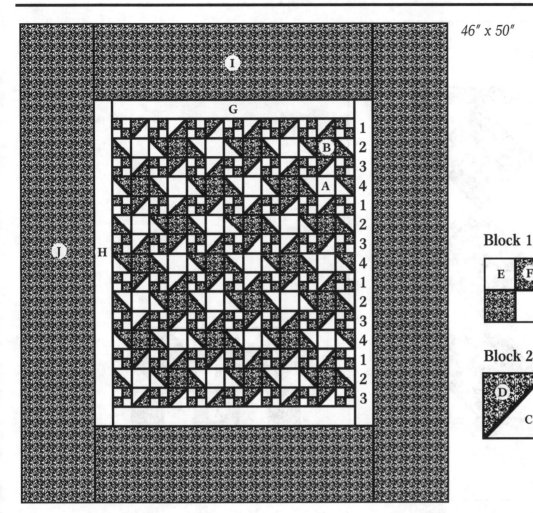

*46" x 50"*

**Block 1**

E | F

**Block 2**

D
C

*Measurements given with seam allowances.*

A — 2¹/2" x 2¹/2"; cut 21
B — 2¹/2" x 2¹/2"; cut 21
C — 2⁷/8" x 2⁷/8"; cut 49; then cut in half diagonally
D — 2⁷/8" x 2⁷/8"; cut 49; then cut in half diagonally
E — 1¹/2" x 1¹/2"; cut 112
F — 1¹/2" x 1¹/2"; cut 112
G — 2¹/2" x 26¹/2"; cut 2
H — 2¹/2" x 34¹/2"; cut 2
I — 8¹/2" x 30¹/2"; cut 2
J — 8¹/2" x 50¹/2"; cut 2

## Assembly Instructions:

1. To create Block 1:

   A. Sew a Template F to a Template E. Repeat 111 times (112 strips total).

   B. Sew an E/F Strip to an F/E strip to form block. Repeat 55 times (56 blocks total).

2. To create Block 2:

   A. Sew long side of a Template C to the long side of a Template D. Repeat 96 times (97 blocks total).

3. Sew together Row One, working from left to right. Repeat 3 times (4 strips total).

4. Sew together Row Two, working from left to right. Repeat 3 times (4 strips total).

5. Sew together Row Three, working from left to right. Repeat 3 times (4 strips total).

6. Sew together Row Four, working from left to right. Repeat 2 times (3 strips total).

7. Sew Rows together from top to bottom.

8. Follow Border Application Diagram on page 11 to complete your quilt, using templates G through J.

## Fabric Requirements

☐ — 1¹/4 yds.

▓ — 3³/4 yds.

Backing — If using horizontal seams—2³/4 yds.
              If using vertical seams—2¹/2 yds.
Batting— 51" x 55"

79

# Rolling Stone

*45$^1$/$_2$" x 58$^1$/$_2$"*

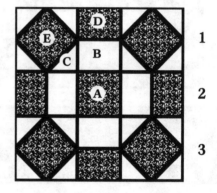

*Measurements given with seam allowances.*

A — Template given; cut 6
B — Template given; cut 24
C — Template given; cut 96
D — Template given; cut 24
E — Template given; cut 24
F — 9$^1$/$_2$" x 9$^1$/$_2$"; cut 2
G — 9$^7$/$_8$" x 9$^7$/$_8$"; cut 3; cut in half diagonally
H — 7$^1$/$_4$" x 7$^1$/$_4$"; cut 2; then cut in half diagonally
I — 2$^1$/$_2$" x 26"; cut 2
J — 2$^1$/$_2$" x 42$^5$/$_8$"; cut 2
K — 8$^1$/$_2$" x 30"; cut 2
L — 8$^1$/$_2$" x 58$^5$/$_8$"; cut 2

## Assembly Instructions:

1. To create one Rolling Stone Block:

A. Sew a Template C to each side of Template E. Repeat 23 times (24 blocks total).

B. Sew a Template D to a Template B. Repeat 23 times (24 strips total).

C. Sew together Row 1, working from left to right.

D. Sew together Row 2, working from left to right.

E. Sew together Row 3, working from left to right.

F. Sew Row 1 to Row 2. Sew Row 3 to Row 2 to create block.

G. Repeat steps 1A through 1F 5 more times (6 blocks total).

2. See How to Assemble Your Quilt, Diagram 2, page 10.

3. Follow Border Application Diagram on page 11 to complete your quilt, using Templates I through L.

## Fabric Requirements

— 3$^7$/$_8$ yds.

— $^3$/$_4$ yd.

Backing — If using horizontal seams—3$^1$/$_4$ yds.
          If using vertical seams—2$^1$/$_2$ yds.
Batting— 50" x 63"

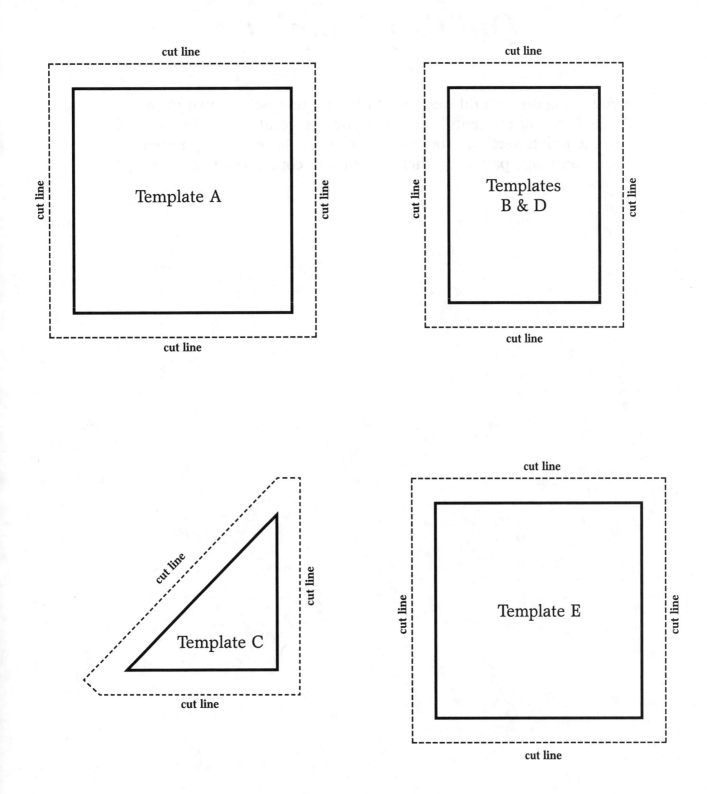

81

# Quilting Templates

Following are several traditional quilting templates given in full size. Many of the templates extend over several pages. To use, pull out template section. Match corresponding letters along dotted lines and tape pages together to form the completed template.

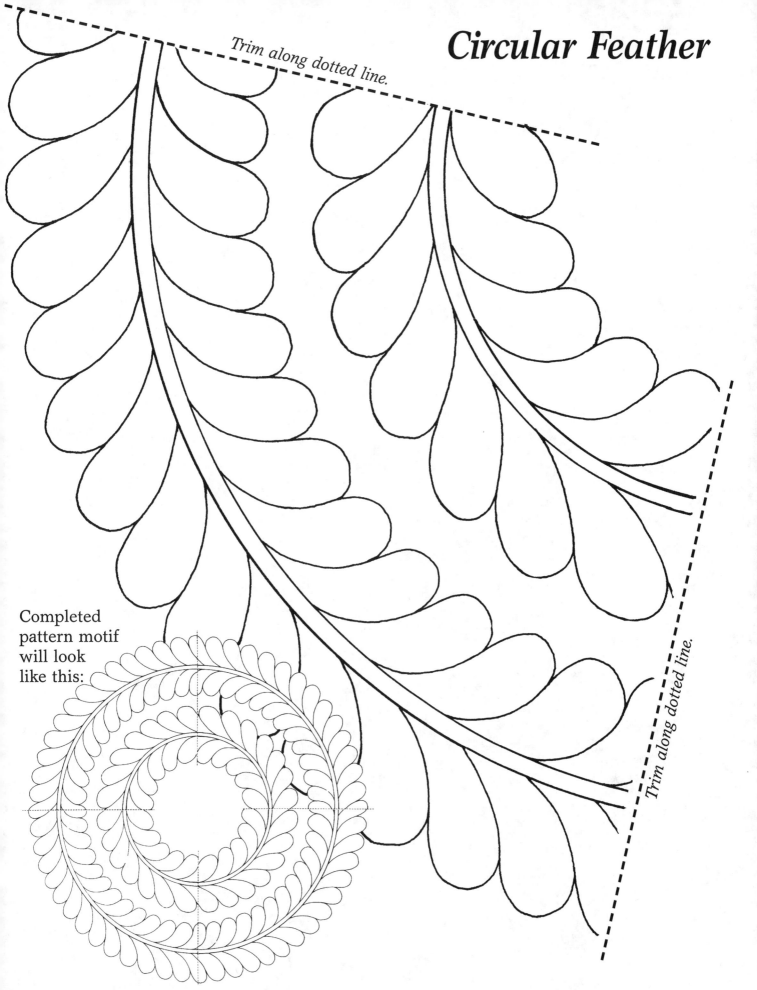

Trim along dotted line.

# Circular Feather

Trim along dotted line.

Completed
pattern motif
will look
like this:

# Triangular Rose—i.

Completed pattern motif will look like this:

To create finished template, match pattern along dotted lines, and tape.

*Trim along dotted line.*

# Triangular Rose—ii.

*Trim along dotted line.*

- - - - - - - - - - - - - - - - - - - - - - - - - - - - - - - - - - - - - - -

## Floral Corner A

# Feather Border—i.

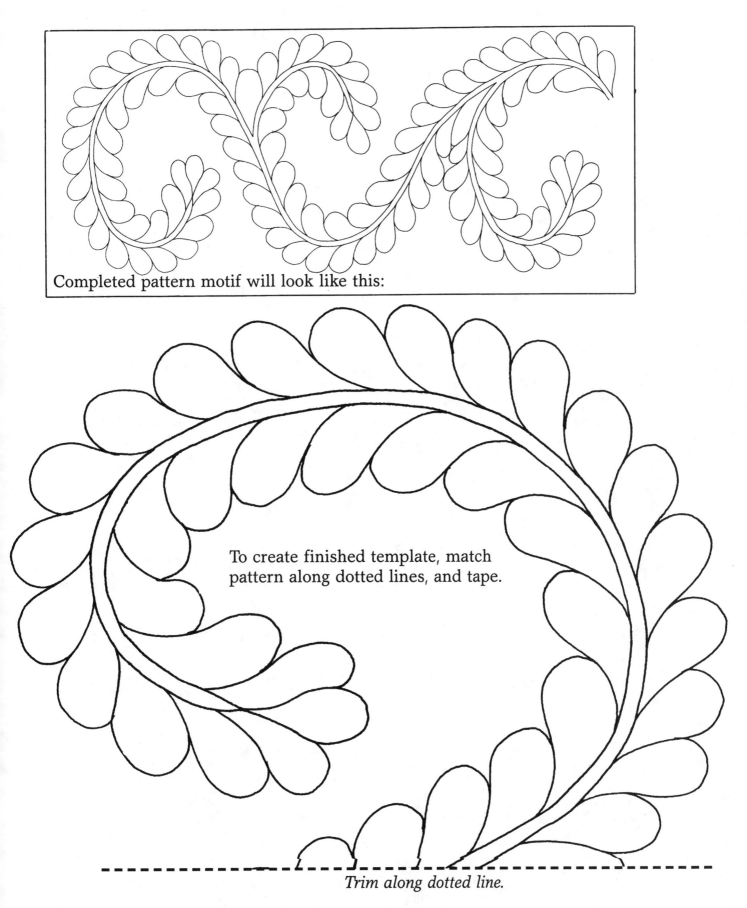

Completed pattern motif will look like this:

To create finished template, match
pattern along dotted lines, and tape.

*Trim along dotted line.*

# Feather Border—ii.

*Trim along dotted line.*

*Trim along dotted line.*

# Feather Border—iii.

*Trim along dotted line.*

**Ivy Leaf**

**Floral Corner B**

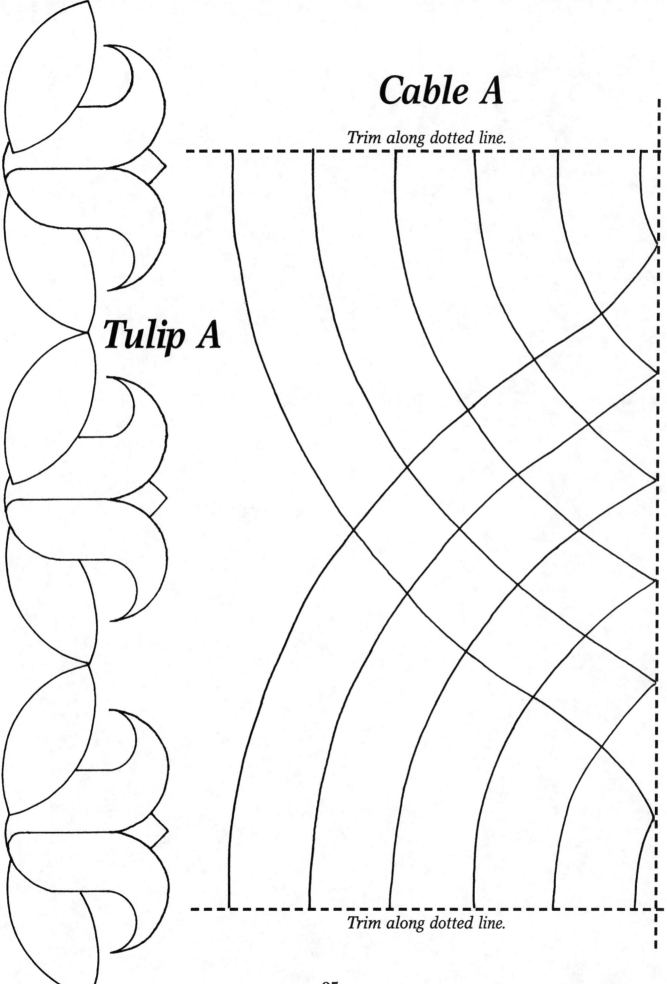

# Cable A

*Trim along dotted line.*

# Tulip A

*Trim along dotted line.*

# Cable B

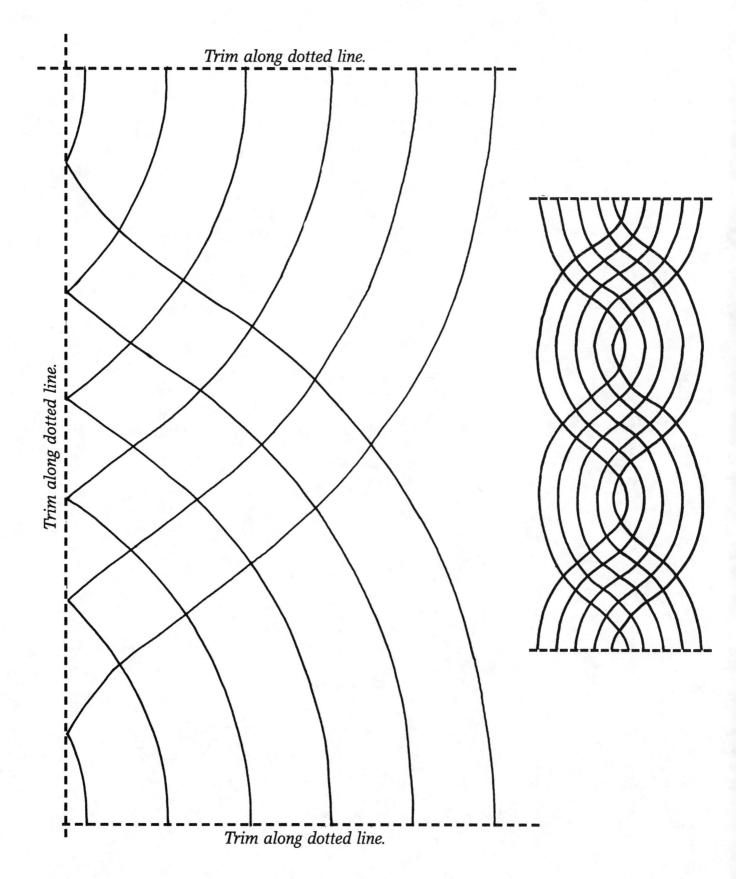

Trim along dotted line.

Trim along dotted line.

Trim along dotted line.

97

*Tulip B*

*Grapes
with
Leaves*

99

# Pumpkin Seed

# Floral Border Design

# Dogwood

# Fan A

# Basket with Tulip—i.

*Trim along dotted line.*

103

# Basket with Tulip—ii.

*Trim along dotted line.*

## Leaves

# Floral Corner D—i.

**Fruit**

*Trim along dotted line.*

# Floral Corner D—ii.

*Trim along dotted line.*

## Baskets

# Feather Heart with Cross-Hatching

# Fan B

# Diamond

# Scalloped Border—i.

*Trim along dotted line.*

# Squares—i.

# Squares—ii.

*Trim along dotted line.*

# Readings and Sources

## Cross-Reference

Pellman, Rachel and Kenneth. **Amish Crib Quilts.** Good Books, Intercourse, Pennsylvania, 1985.

## About Amish Quilts

Bishop, Robert and Elizabeth Safanda. **A Gallery of Amish Quilts.** E. P. Dutton and Company, Inc., New York, New York, 1976.

Granick, Eve Wheatcroft. **The Amish Quilt.** Good Books, Intercourse, Pennsylvania, 1989.

Haders, Phyllis. **Sunshine and Shadow: The Amish and Their Quilts.** Universe Books, New York, New York, 1976.

Horton, Roberta. **Amish Adventure.** C & T Publishing, Lafayette, California, 1983.

Lawson, Suzy. **Amish Inspirations.** Amity Publications, Cottage Grove, Oregon, 1982

Pellman, Rachel T. **Amish Quilt Patterns.** Good Books, Intercourse, Pennsylvania, 1998.

Pellman, Rachel and Jan Steffy. **Patterns for Making Amish Dolls and Doll Clothes.** Good Books, Intercourse, Pennsylvania, 1987.

Pellman, Rachel T. and Joanne Ranck. **Quilts Among the Plain People.** Good Books, Intercourse, Pennsylvania, 1981.

Pellman, Rachel and Kenneth. **Amish Doll Quilts, Dolls, and Other Playthings.** Good Books, Intercourse, Pennsylvania, 1986.

Pellman, Rachel and Kenneth. **A Treasury of Amish Quilts.** Good Books, Intercourse, Pennsylvania, 1990.

Pellman, Rachel and Kenneth. **The World of Amish Quilts.** Good Books, Intercourse, Pennsylvania, 1998.

Pottinger, David. **Quilts from the Indiana Amish.** E. P. Dutton, Inc., New York, New York, 1983.

## About Other Quilts

Pellman, Rachel T. **Tips for Quilters.** Good Books, Intercourse, Pennsylvania, 1993.

## About the Amish

Budget, The. Sugarcreek, Ohio, 1890. A weekly newspaper serving the Amish and Mennonite communities.

Devoted Christian's Prayer Book. Pathway Publishing House, Aylmer, Ontario, 1967.

Family Life. Amish periodical published monthly. Pathway Publishing House, Aylmer, Ontario.

Good, Merle. **An Amish Portrait: Song of a People.** Good Books, Intercourse, Pennsylvania, 1993.

Good, Merle. **Who Are the Amish?** Good Books, Intercourse, Pennsylvania, 1985.

Good, Merle and Phyllis Good. **20 Most Asked Questions about the Amish and Mennonites.** Good Books, Lancaster, Pennsylvania, 1995.

Good, Phyllis Pellman. **The Best of Amish Cooking.** Good Books, Intercourse, Pennsylvania, 1988.

Good, Phyllis Pellman. **Delicious Amish Recipes.** Good Books, Intercourse, Pennsylvania, 1997.

Good, Phyllis Pellman and Rachel Thomas Pellman. **From Amish and Mennonite Kitchens.** Good Books, Intercourse, Pennsylvania, 1984.

Hostetler, John A. **Amish Life.** Herald Press, Scottdale, Pennsylvania, 1983.

Hostetler, John A. **Amish Society.** Johns Hopkins University Press, Baltimore, Maryland, 1993.

Kaiser, Grace H. **Dr. Frau: A Woman Doctor Among the Amish.** Good Books, Intercourse, Pennsylvania, 1997.

Kraybill, Donald B. **The Puzzles of Amish Life.** Good Books, Intercourse, Pennsylvania, 1995.

Nolt, Steven. **A History of the Amish.** Good Books, Intercourse, Pennsylvania, 1992.

Scott, Stephen. **Living Without Electricity.** Good Books, Intercourse, Pennsylvania, 1990.

Scott, Stephen. **Why Do They Dress That Way?** Good Books, Intercourse, Pennsylvania, 1997.

Stoltzfus, Louise. **Amish Women.** Good Books, Intercourse, Pennsylvania, 1994.

# Index

# About the Author

Rachel Thomas Pellman designs quilts and quilt kits and lectures widely about quilts. She and her husband Kenneth are co-authors of *Amish Crib Quilts*, a companion book to *Small Amish Quilt Patterns*, as well as *A Treasury of Amish Quilts* and *The World of Amish Quilts*. The Pellmans live near Lancaster, Pennsylvania.